GCATI

Wardley Mapping Notebook

November 2020 Edition

First Printing, 2020

ISBN 978-1-913805-24-1

gcati.org

Phases of Evolution

Stage of Evolution		I	II	III	IV
x-axis labels (types of capital)	**Activity (used)**	Genesis	Custom	Product (+rental)	Commodity (+utility)
	Data (implied)	Unmodelled	Divergent	Convergent	Modelled
	Practice (implied	Novel	Emerging	Good	Best
	Knowledge (implied)	Concept	Hypothesis	Theory	Universally Accepted
Characteristics					
	Ubiquity	Rare	Slowly increasing	Rapidly increasing	Widespread in the applicable market / ecosystem
	Certainty	Poorly understood / exploring the unknown	Rapid increases in learning / discovery becomes refining	Rapid increases in use / increasing fit for purpose	Commonly understood (in terms of use)
	Publication Types	Describe the wonder of the thing / the discovery of some marvel / a new land / an unknown frontier	Focused on build / construct / awareness and learning / many models of explanation / no accepted forms / a wild west.	Maintenance / operations / installation / comparison between competing forms / feature analysis e.g. merits of one model over another	Focused on use / increasingly an accepted, almost invisible component
General Properties					
	Market	Undefined market	Forming market / an array of competing forms and different models of understanding	Growing market / consolidation to a few competing but more accepted forms.	Mature market / stabilised to an accepted form
	Knowledge management	Uncertain	Learning on use / focused on testing prediction	Learning on operation / using prediction / verification	known / accepted
	Market (Ecosystem) Perception	Chaotic (non linear) / Domain of the "crazy"	Domain of "experts"	Increasing expectation of use / Domain of "professionals"	Ordered (appearance of being linear) / trivial / formula to be applied
	User perception	Different / confusing / exciting / surprising / dangerous	Leading edge / emerging / uncertainty over results	Increasingly common / disappointed if not used or available / feeling left behind	Standard / expected / feeling of shock if not used
	Perception in Indusry	Future source of competitive advantage / unpredictable / unknown	Seen as a competitive advantage / a differential / looking for ROI and case examples	Advantage through implementation / features / this model is better than that	Cost of doing business / accepted / specific defined models
	Focus of value	High future worth but immediate investment	Seeking ways to profit and a ROI / seeking confirmation of value	High profitability per unit / a valuable model / a feeling of understanding / focus on exploitation	High volume / reducing margin / important but invisible / an essential component of something more complex
	Understanding	Poorly understood / unpredictable	Increasing understanding / development of measures	Increasing education / constant refinement of needs / measures	Believed to be well defined / stable / measurable
	Comparison	Constantly changing / a differential / unstable	Learning from others / testing the water / some evidential support	Competing models / feature difference / evidential support	Essential / any advantage is operational / accepted norm
	Failure	High / tolerated / assumed to be wrong	Moderate / unsurprising if wrong but disappointed	Not tolerated / focus on constant improvement / assumed to be in the right direction / resistance to changing the model	Surprised by failure / focus on operational efficiency
	Market action	Gambling / driven by gut	Exploring a "found" value	Market analysis / listening to customers	Metric driven / build what is needed
	Efficiency	Reducing the cost of change (experimentation)	Reducing cost of waste (Learning)	Reducing cost of waste (Learning)	Reducing cost of deviation (Volume)
	Decision Drivers	Heritage / culture	Analysis & synthesis	Analysis & synthesis	Previous experience

Source: Wardley Maps. Topographical intelligence in business

Inertia

Category	Example	Tactic to counter	Counter points and messaging
Disruption of Past Norms	Change of business relationship (loss of social capital)	Vendor Management	Right for its time / Past has evolved / Point to other departments / Lead the charge
	Loss of existing financial or physical capital	Future Planning	Asset write down / Look to sweat and dump or dispose / Point to savings vs increasing running costs of legacy
	Loss of political capital	Modernisation	Emphasis on future agility & efficiency / Make the business aware / Building for the future
	Threat to barriers to entry	Unavoidable Change	Already happening in the market
Transition to the New	Investment in knowledge capital	Training	Cost of acquiring external skills will be high / motivation of staff
	Cost of acquiring new skillsets	Organisational development	Develop capabilities in-house / use hack days / use conferences / create centres of gravity
	Investment in new business relationships	Vendor Management	Developing relationships with the right suppliers / understanding the market
	Changes to governance, management and practices	Awareness of Co-evolution	Practices have to adapt as activities evolve / Point to other past practices
Agency of the New	Suitability	Weak Signals & prior identification	Examine ubiquity vs certainty
	Lack of second sourcing options	Supply Chain Management	Use and development of standards, open source options, limit feature use to reduce lock-in, use of abstraction layers)
	Lack of pricing competition	Market Analysis	Single or multiple vendors, examine switching costs, use of brokers
	Loss of strategic control	Strategic Planning	Examine buyer / supplier relationship, understand the market is commoditising and is now a volume operations game)
Business Model	Declining unit value	Awareness of Evolution	Avoid death spiral, Look at alternative opportunities e.g. ecosystem use
	Data for Past Success counteracts	Portfolio Management	Risk Mitigation, look at disposal / spin-off
	Resistance from rewards and culture	Human Resources	Higher rewards for adaptation, Education, Promote situational awareness
	External financial markets reinforce existing models	Analyst Relationships	Spinning a future story

Source: Wardley Maps. Topographical intelligence in business

Phases of Evolution

Class / Phase	Type I	Type 2	Type 3	Type 3b	Type 4	Type 4b
Key descriptive terms	Wonder & exploration	Construction, awareness & validation	Operation, maintenance, feature differentiation & refinement		Dominated by use, increasingly an invisible sub component of other systems	
Theme	**Uncharted**	**Transitional**			**Industrialised**	
Properties	Uncertain, rare, risky, future worth, differential, chaotic, unmeasured, poorly understood, changing, deviates from past				Certain, common, predictable, cost of doing business, accepted, measured, standard, defined, static, known, essential	
Activities	Genesis	Custom Built	Product (Rental Service)		Commodity (Utility Service)	
Practices	Novel	Emerging	Good		Best	
Data	Unmodelled	Divergent	Convergent		Modelled	
Knowledge	Concept	Hypothesis	Theory		Universally Accepted	

Source: Wardley Maps. Topographical intelligence in business

Uncharted

Industrialised

Visible

Value Chain

Invisible

Genesis

Custom Built

Product (+ rental)

Commodity (+ utility)

Evolution

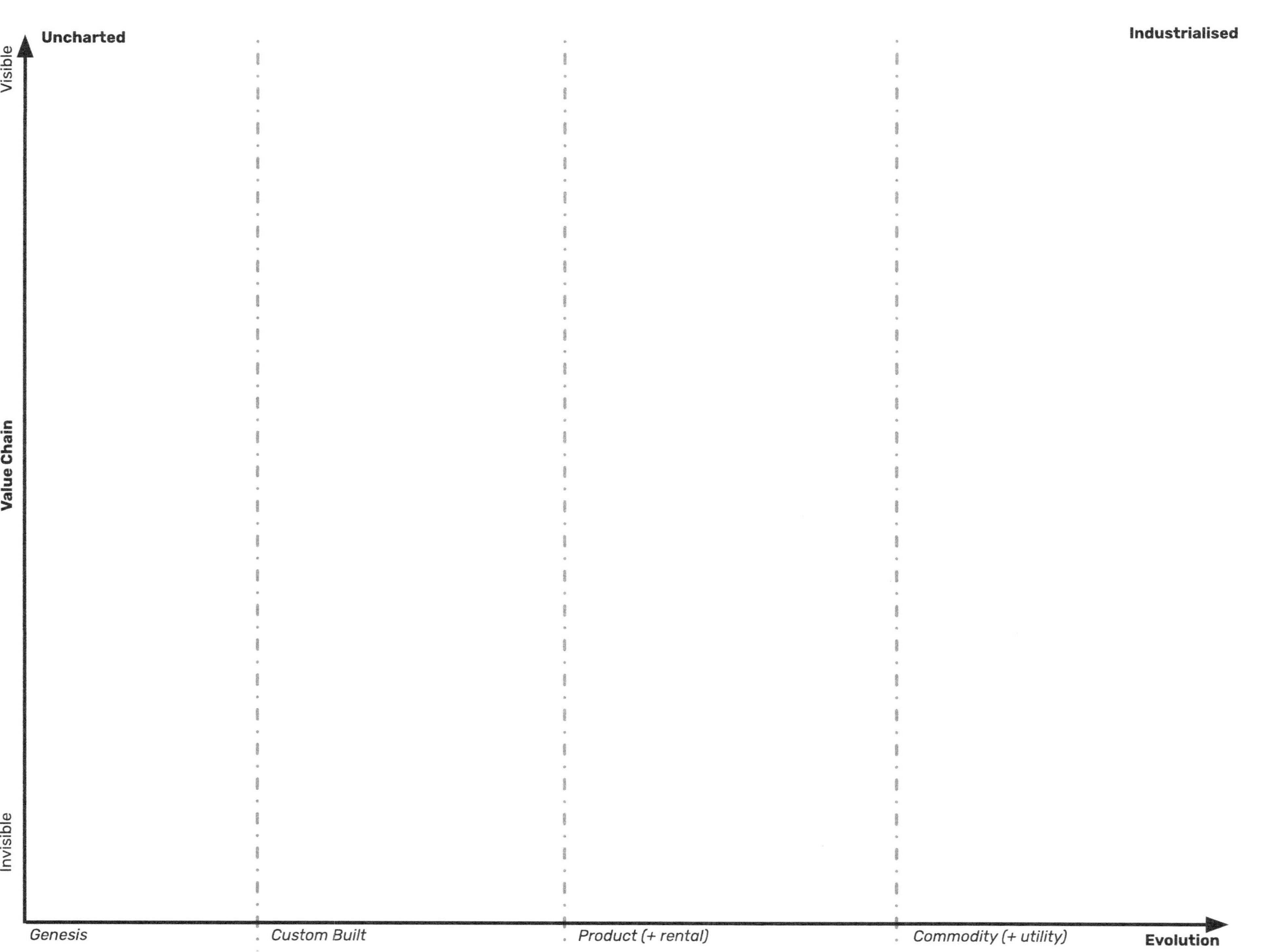
Uncharted
Industrialised
Visible
Value Chain
Invisible
Genesis
Custom Built
Product (+ rental)
Commodity (+ utility)
Evolution

Uncharted

Industrialised

Visible

Value Chain

Invisible

Genesis

Custom Built

Product (+ rental)

Commodity (+ utility)

Evolution

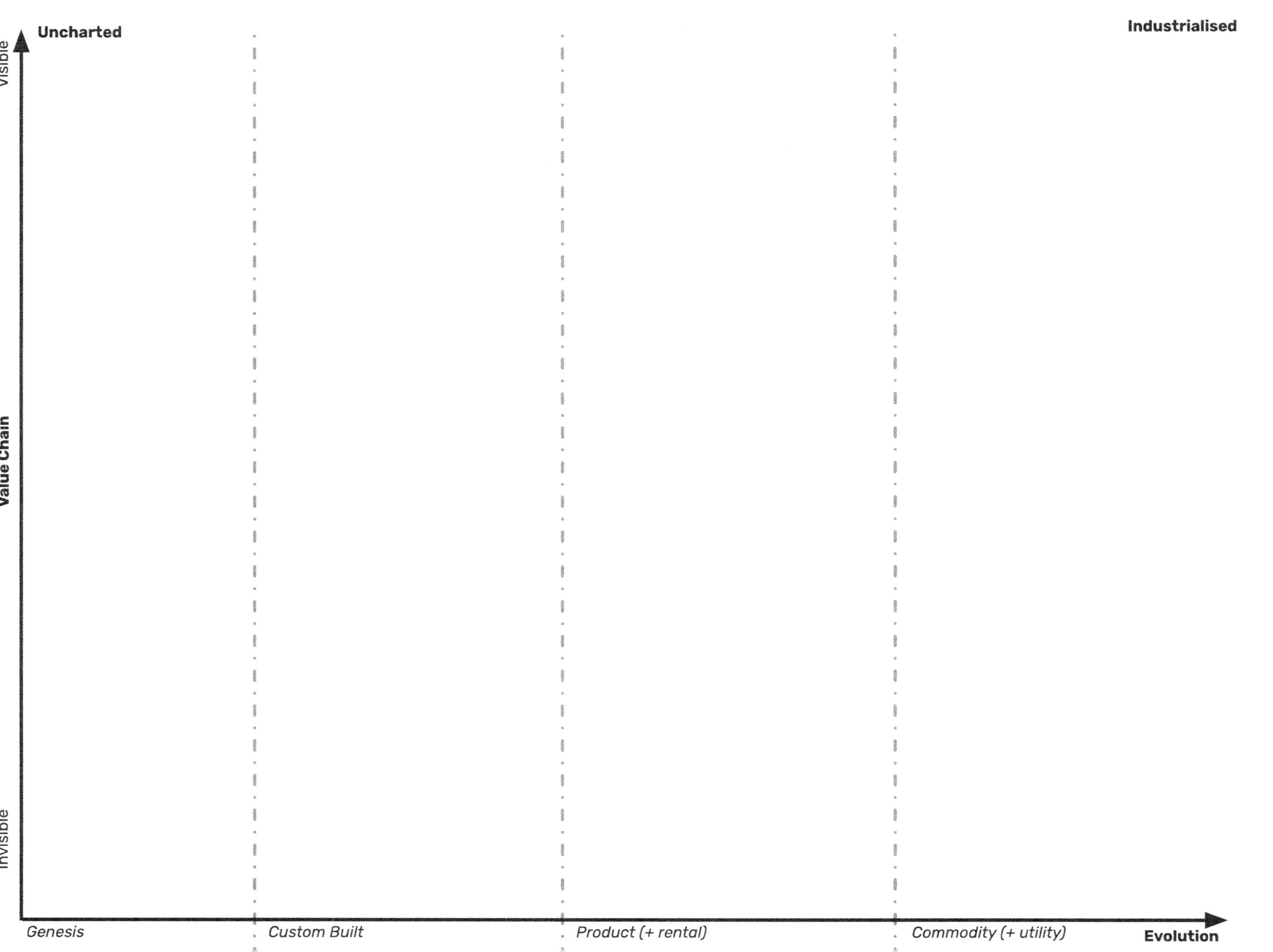
Uncharted
Industrialised
Visible
Value Chain
Invisible
Genesis
Custom Built
Product (+ rental)
Commodity (+ utility)
Evolution

Uncharted
Industrialised
Visible
Value Chain
Invisible
Genesis
Custom Built
Product (+ rental)
Commodity (+ utility)
Evolution

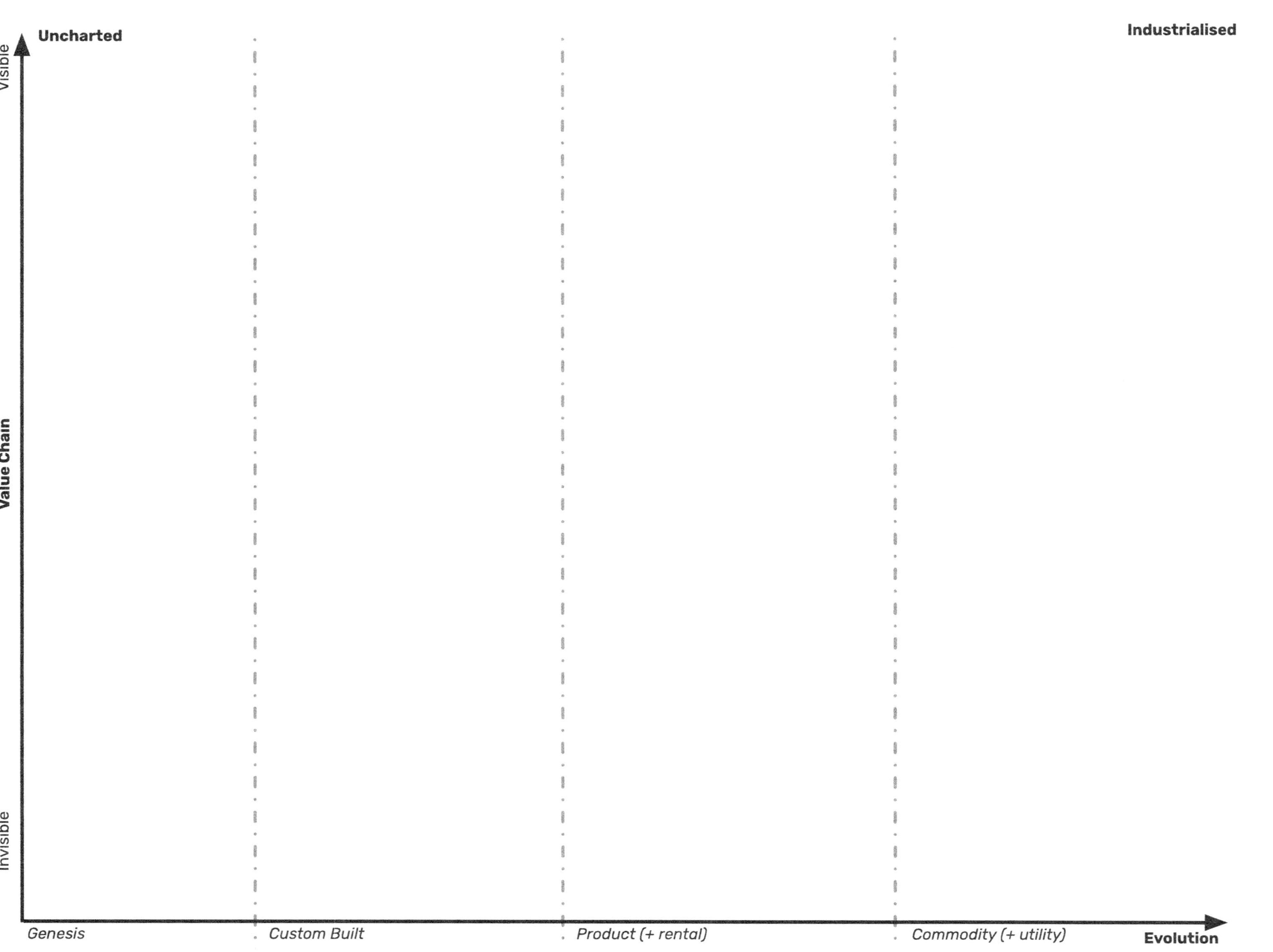
Uncharted
Industrialised
Visible
Value Chain
Invisible
Genesis
Custom Built
Product (+ rental)
Commodity (+ utility)
Evolution

Uncharted

Industrialised

Visible

Value Chain

Invisible

Genesis

Custom Built

Product (+ rental)

Commodity (+ utility)

Evolution

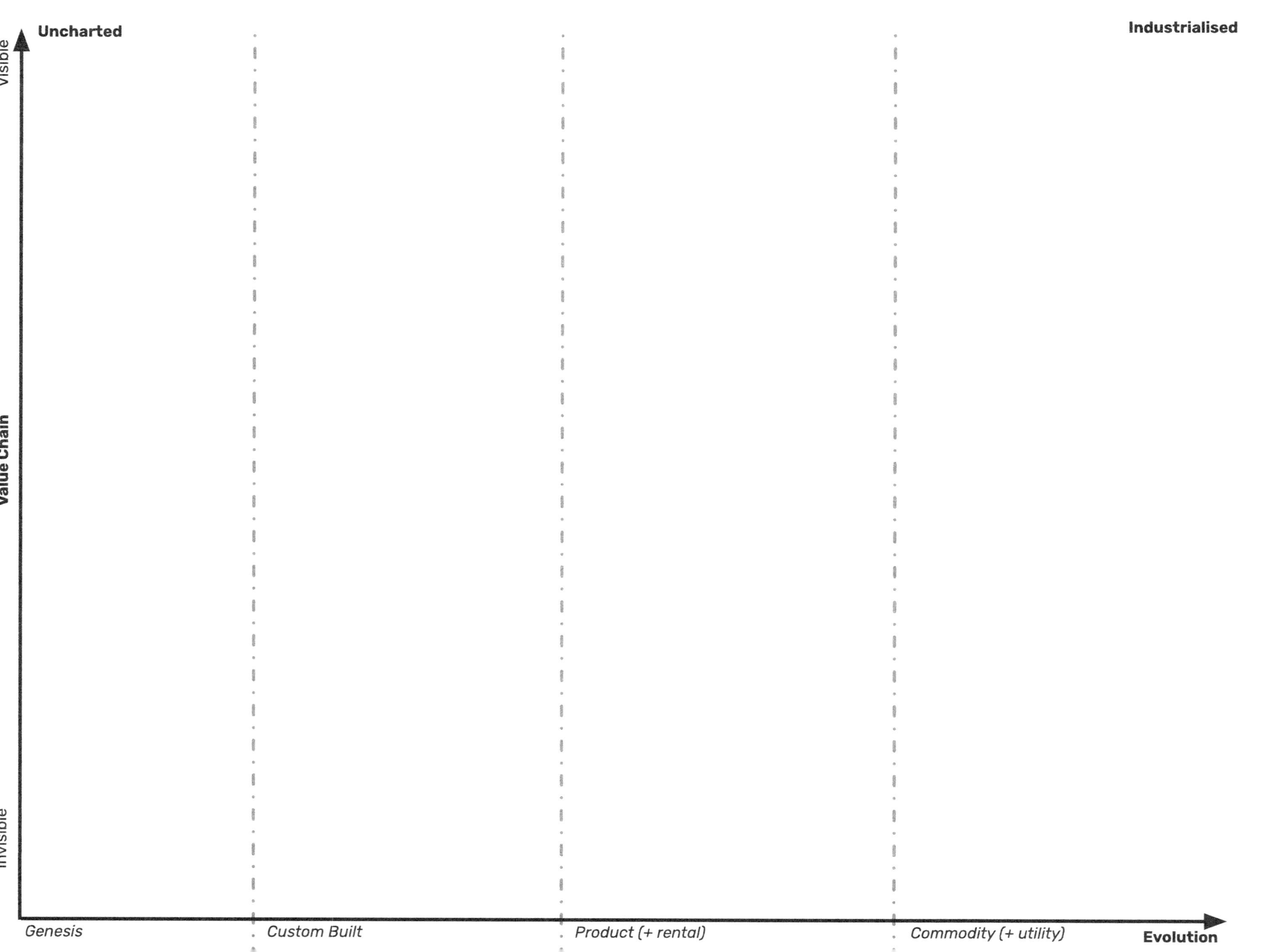
Uncharted
Industrialised
Visible
Value Chain
Invisible
Genesis
Custom Built
Product (+ rental)
Commodity (+ utility)
Evolution

Uncharted

Industrialised

Visible

Value Chain

Invisible

Genesis

Custom Built

Product (+ rental)

Commodity (+ utility)

Evolution

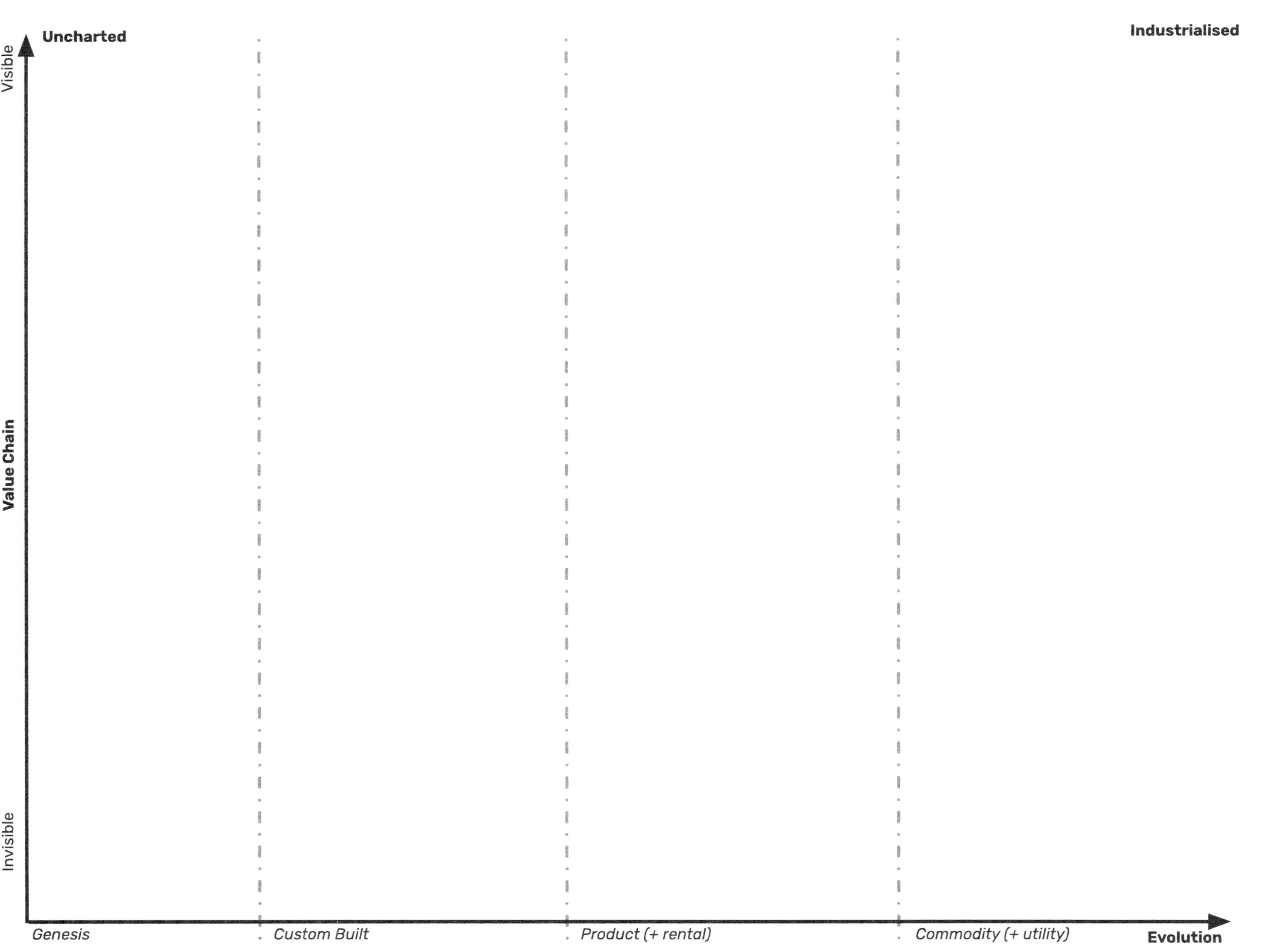
Uncharted
Industrialised
Visible
Value Chain
Invisible
Genesis
Custom Built
Product (+ rental)
Commodity (+ utility)
Evolution

Uncharted

Industrialised

Visible

Value Chain

Invisible

Genesis

Custom Built

Product (+ rental)

Commodity (+ utility)

Evolution

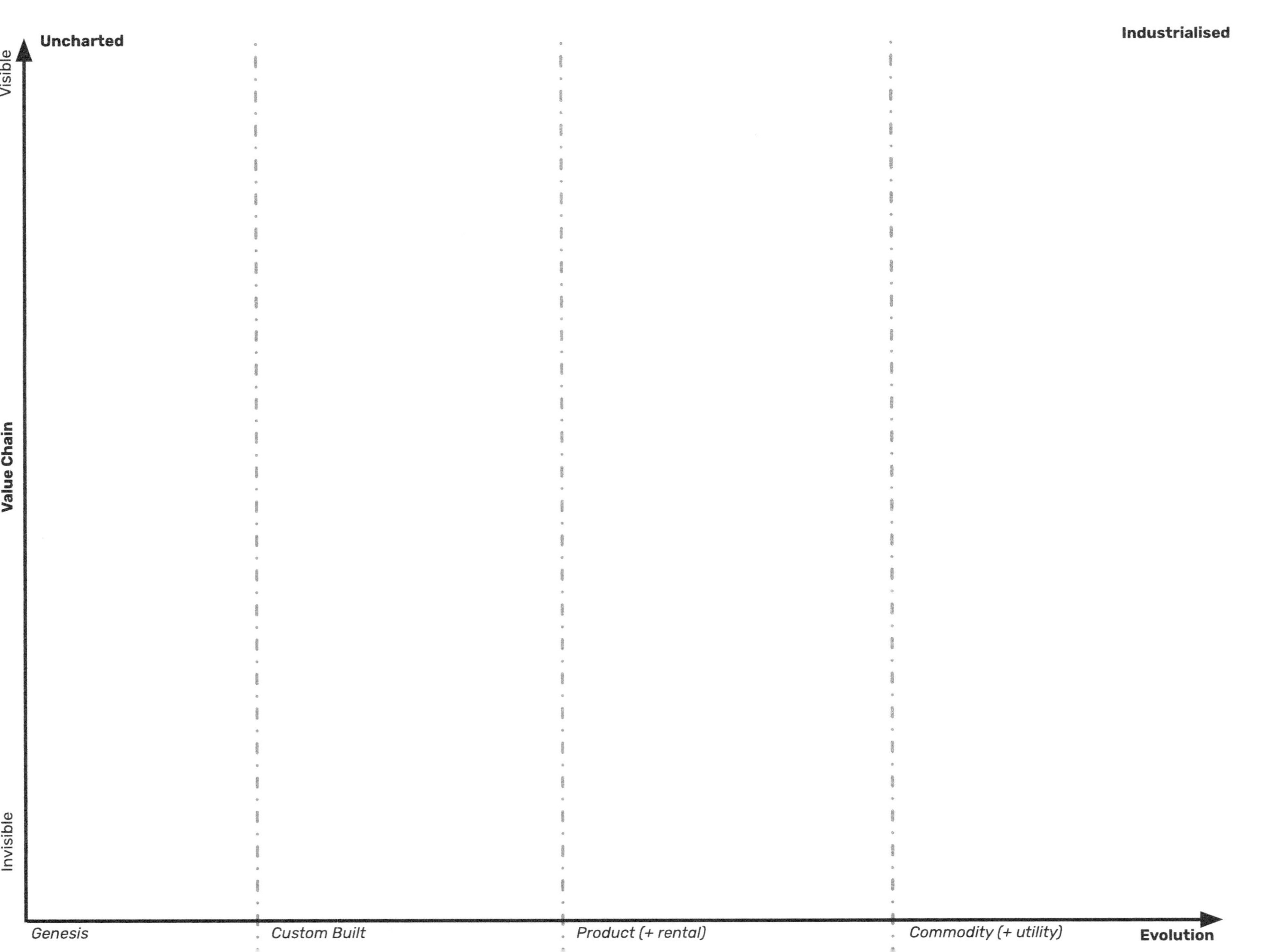
Uncharted
Industrialised
Visible
Value Chain
Invisible
Genesis
Custom Built
Product (+ rental)
Commodity (+ utility)
Evolution

Uncharted

Industrialised

Visible

Value Chain

Invisible

Genesis *Custom Built* *Product (+ rental)* *Commodity (+ utility)* **Evolution**

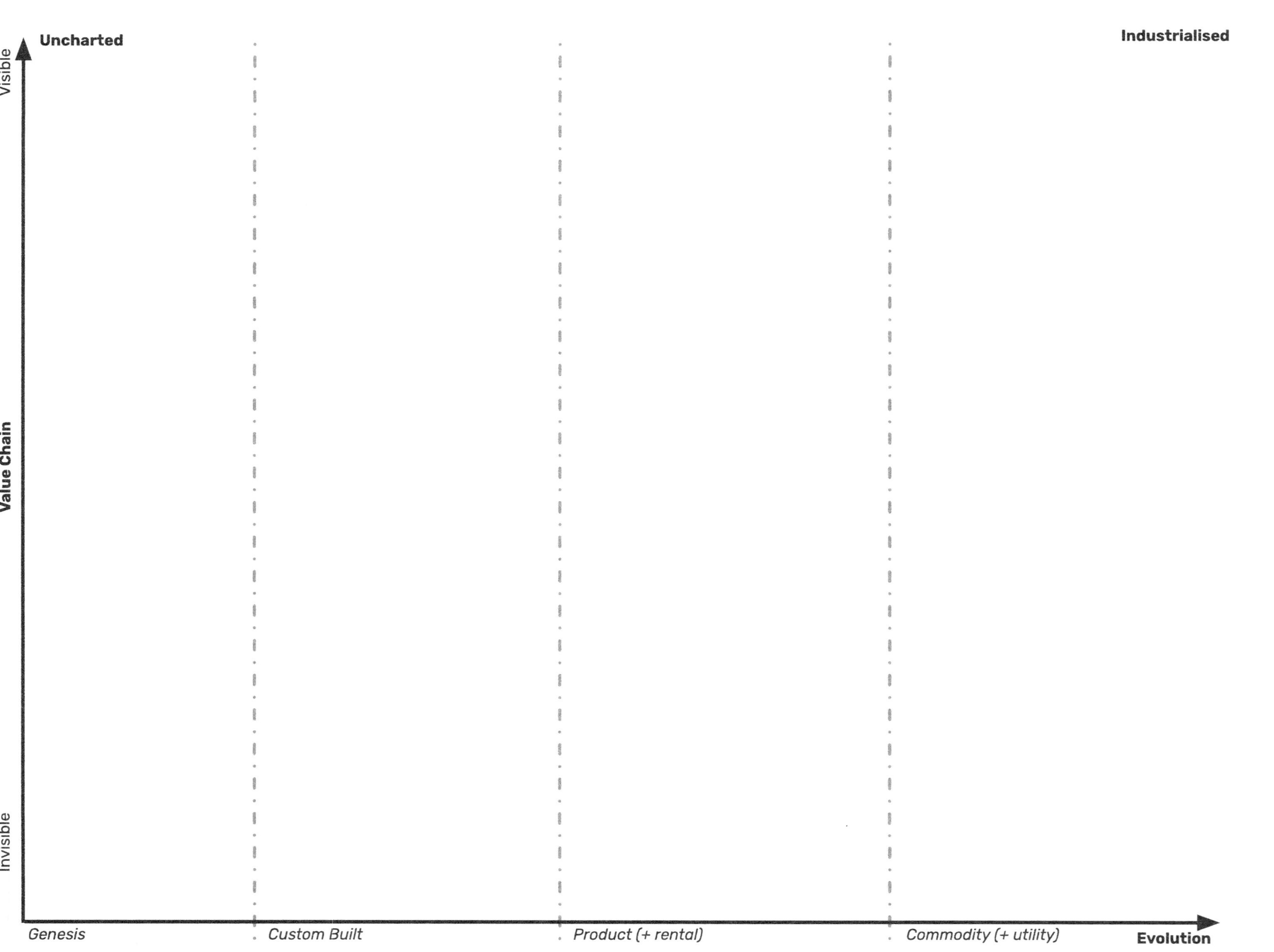
Uncharted
Industrialised
Visible
Value Chain
Invisible
Genesis
Custom Built
Product (+ rental)
Commodity (+ utility)
Evolution

Uncharted

Industrialised

Visible

Value Chain

Invisible

Genesis

Custom Built

Product (+ rental)

Commodity (+ utility)

Evolution

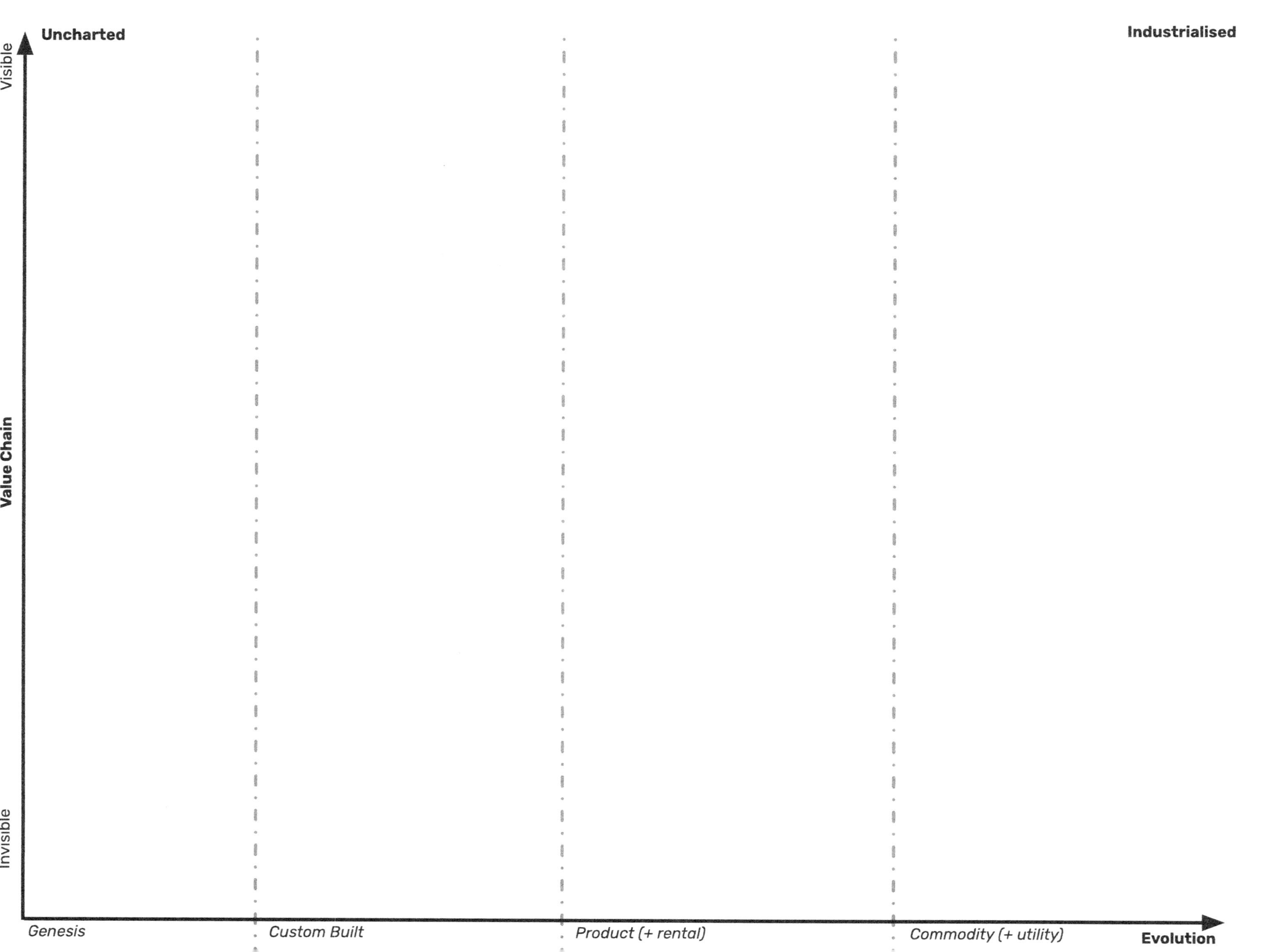
Uncharted
Industrialised
Visible
Value Chain
Invisible
Genesis
Custom Built
Product (+ rental)
Commodity (+ utility)
Evolution

Uncharted

Industrialised

Visible

Value Chain

Invisible

Genesis

Custom Built

Product (+ rental)

Commodity (+ utility)

Evolution

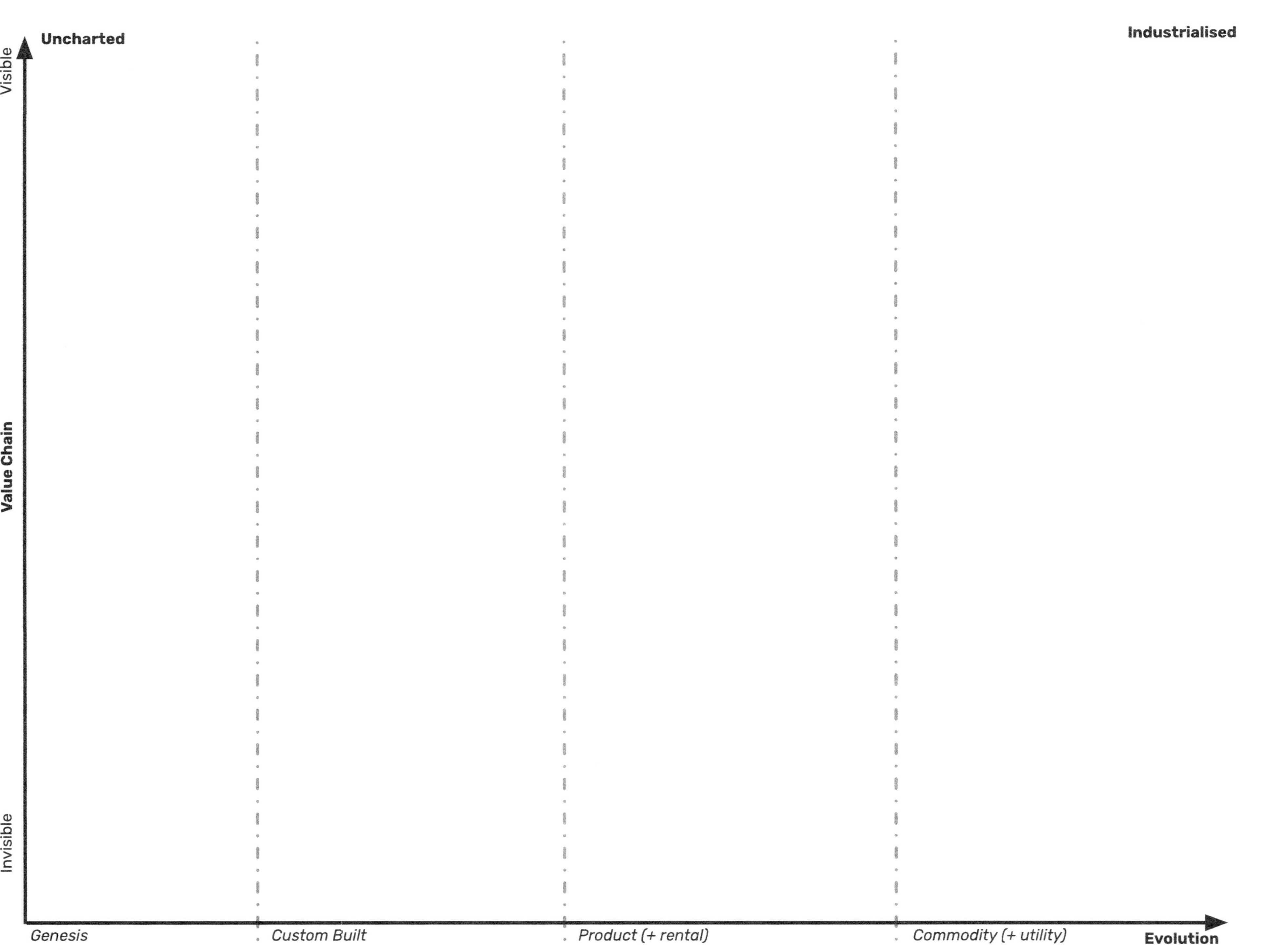
Uncharted
Industrialised
Visible
Value Chain
Invisible
Genesis
Custom Built
Product (+ rental)
Commodity (+ utility)
Evolution

Uncharted

Industrialised

Visible

Value Chain

Invisible

Genesis

Custom Built

Product (+ rental)

Commodity (+ utility)

Evolution

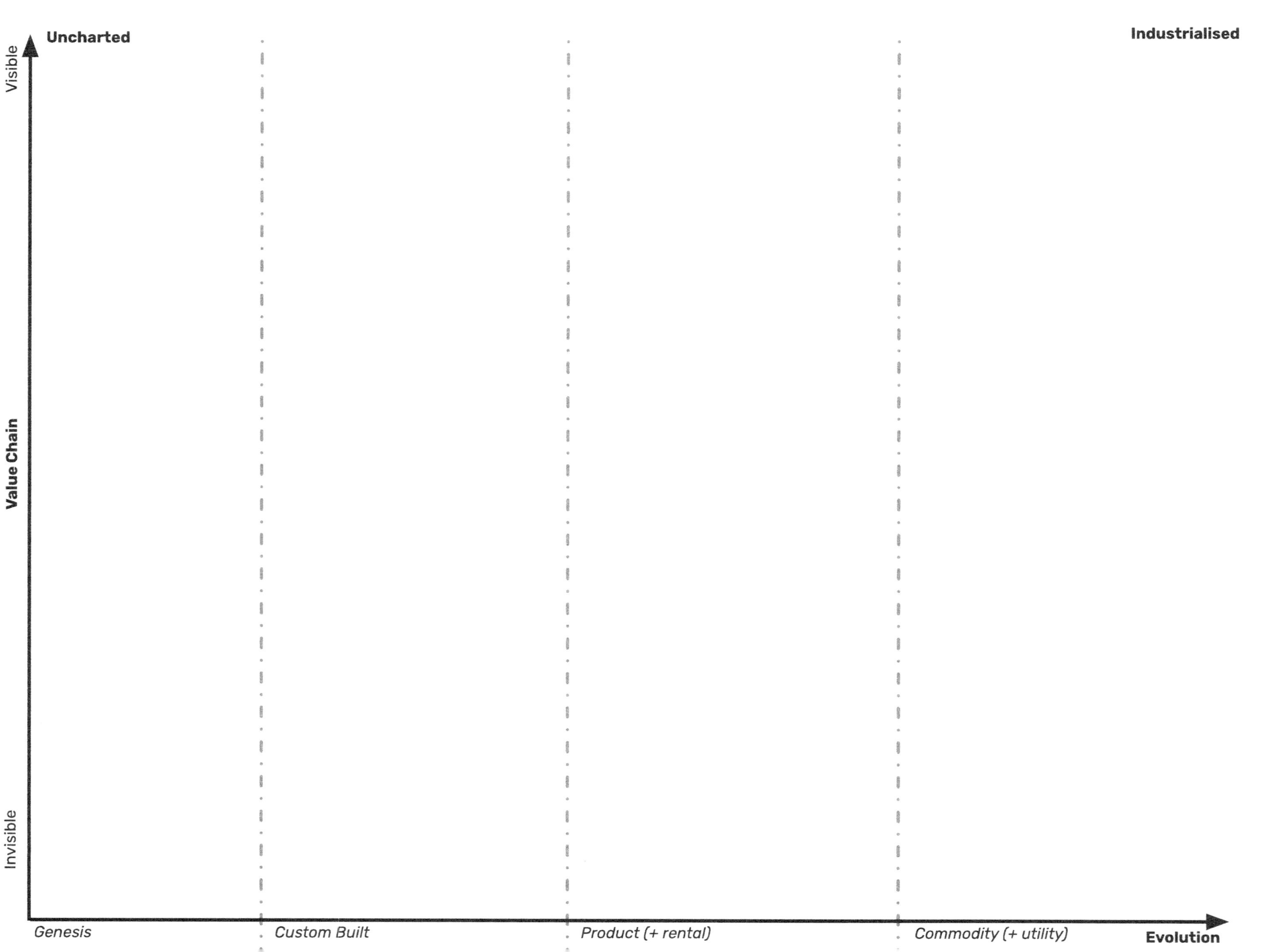
Uncharted
Industrialised
Visible
Value Chain
Invisible
Genesis
Custom Built
Product (+ rental)
Commodity (+ utility)
Evolution

Uncharted

Industrialised

Visible

Value Chain

Invisible

Genesis *Custom Built* *Product (+ rental)* *Commodity (+ utility)*

Evolution

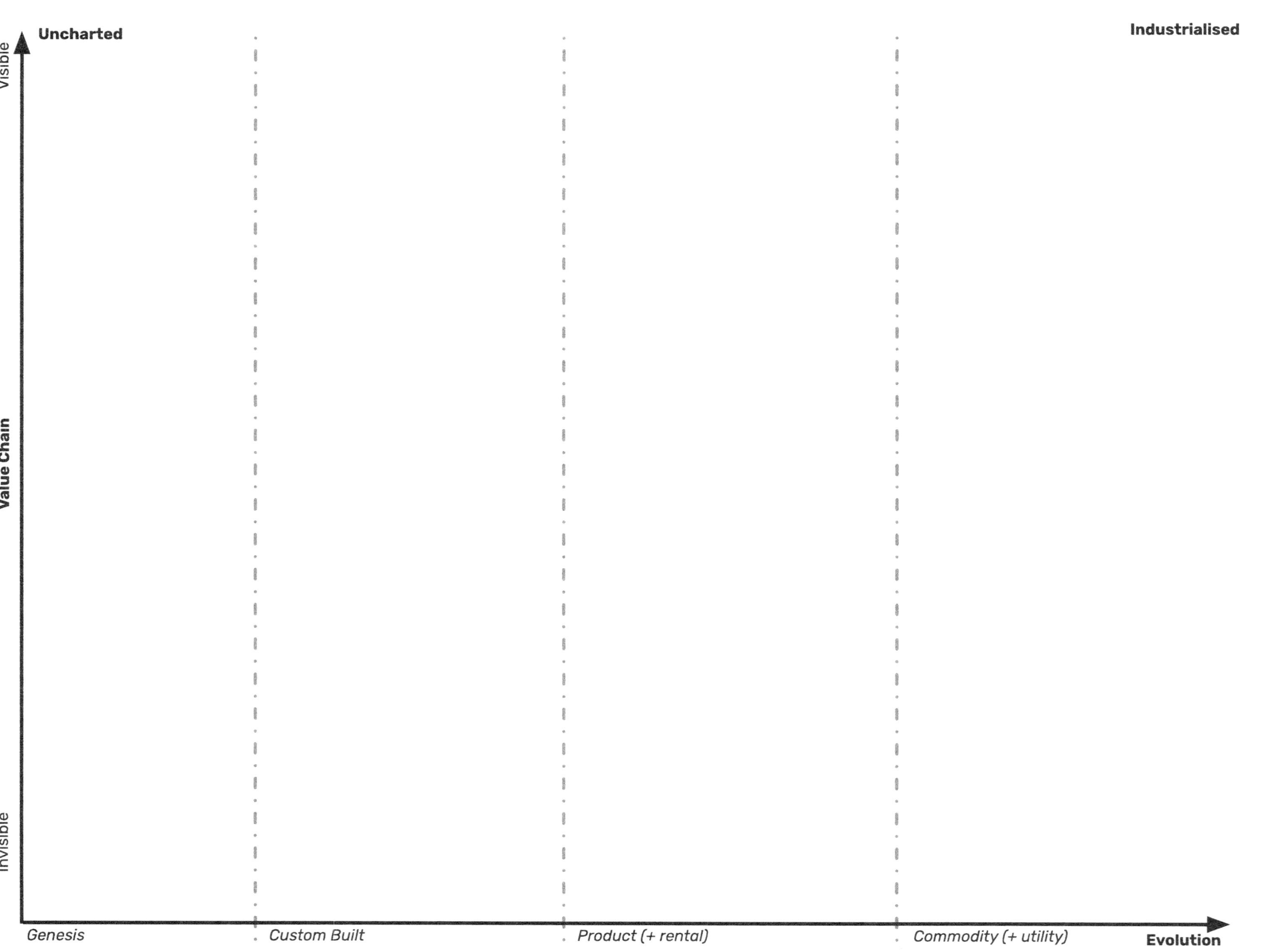
Uncharted
Industrialised
Visible
Value Chain
Invisible
Genesis
Custom Built
Product (+ rental)
Commodity (+ utility)
Evolution

Uncharted

Industrialised

Visible

Value Chain

Invisible

Genesis

Custom Built

Product (+ rental)

Commodity (+ utility)

Evolution

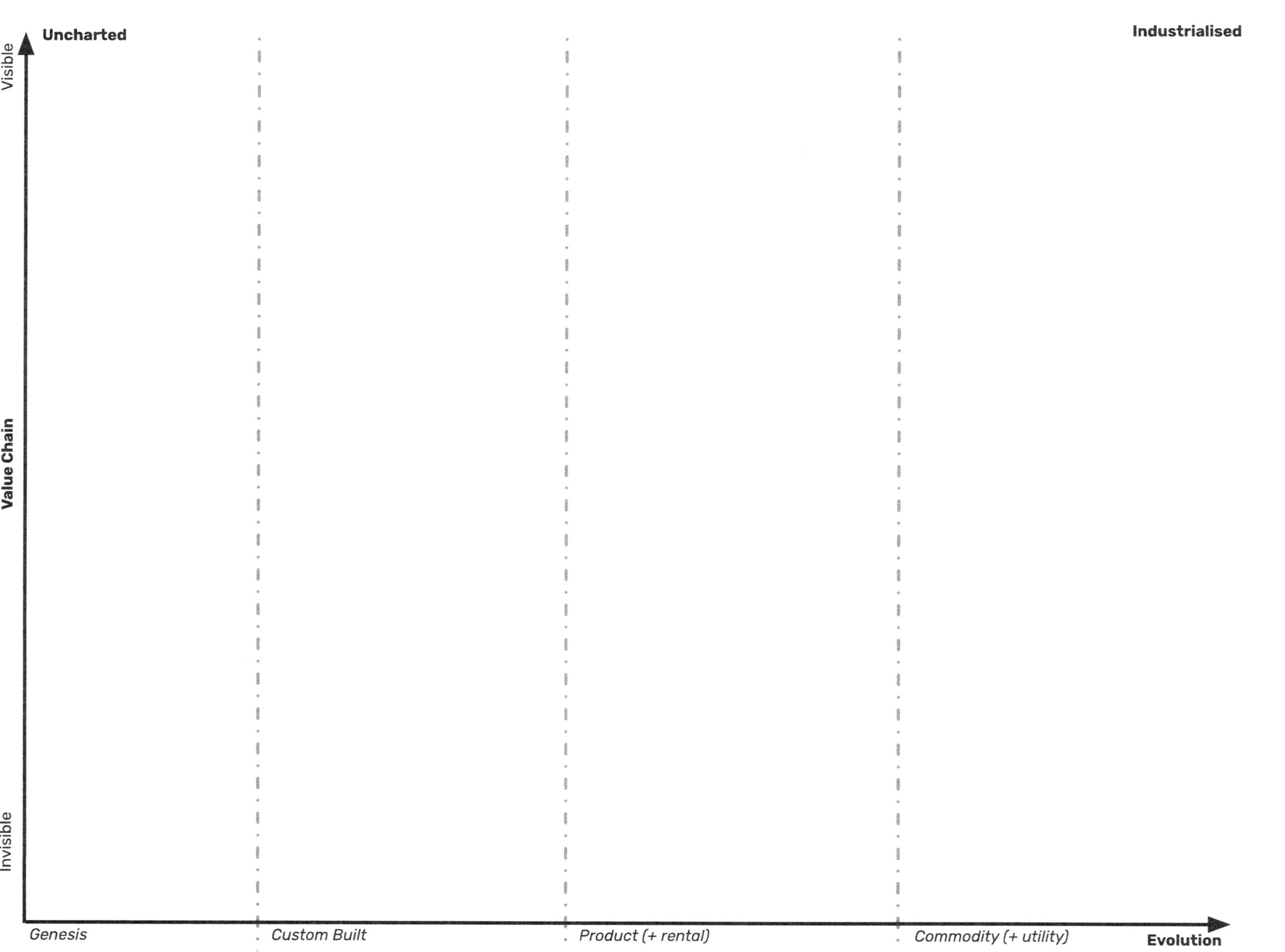
Uncharted
Industrialised
Visible
Value Chain
Invisible
Genesis
Custom Built
Product (+ rental)
Commodity (+ utility)
Evolution

Uncharted
Industrialised
Visible
Value Chain
Invisible
Genesis
Custom Built
Product (+ rental)
Commodity (+ utility)
Evolution

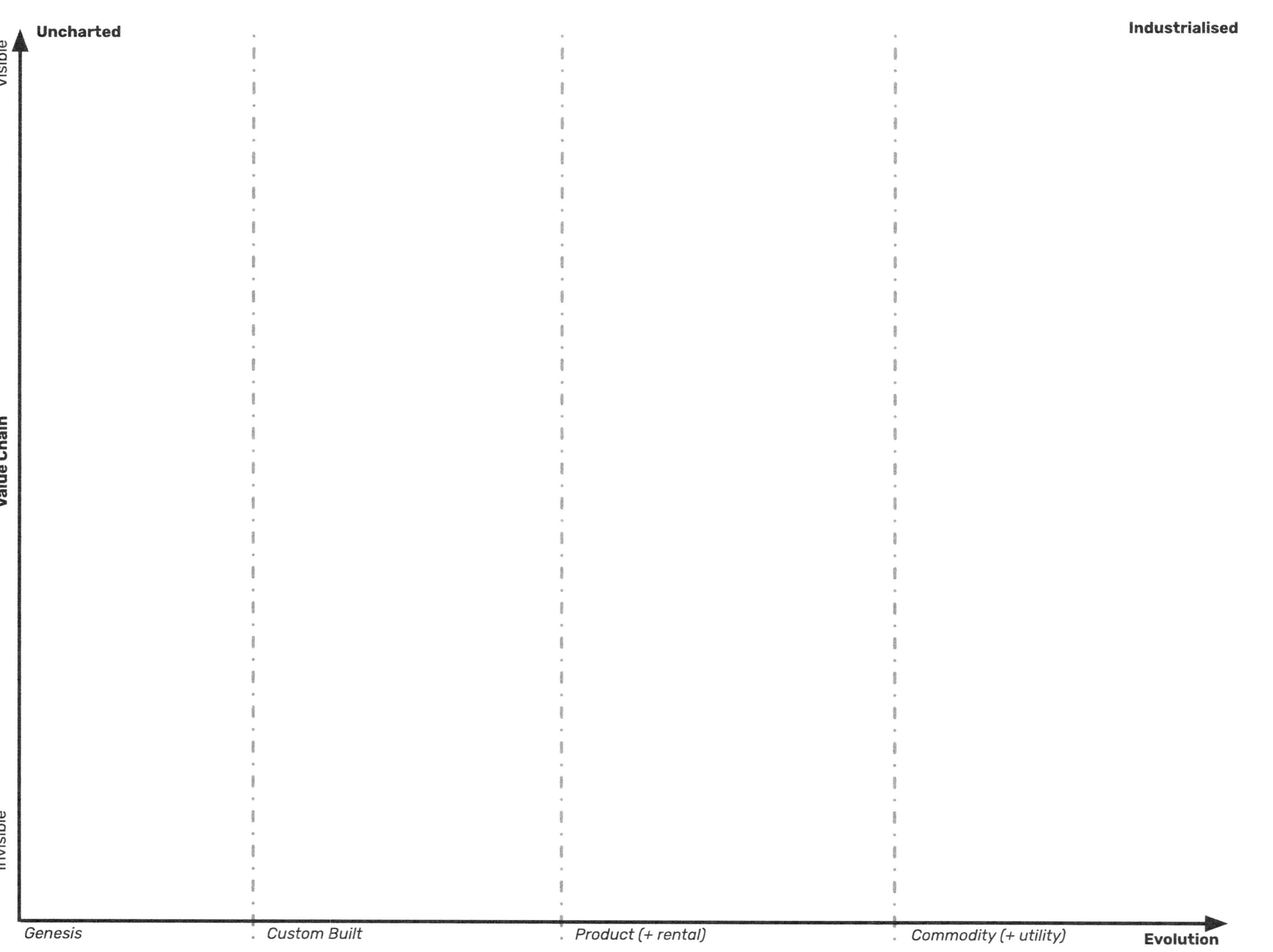
Uncharted
Industrialised
Visible
Value Chain
Invisible
Genesis
Custom Built
Product (+ rental)
Commodity (+ utility)
Evolution

Uncharted **Industrialised**

Value Chain

Visible

Invisible

Genesis *Custom Built* *Product (+ rental)* *Commodity (+ utility)*

Evolution

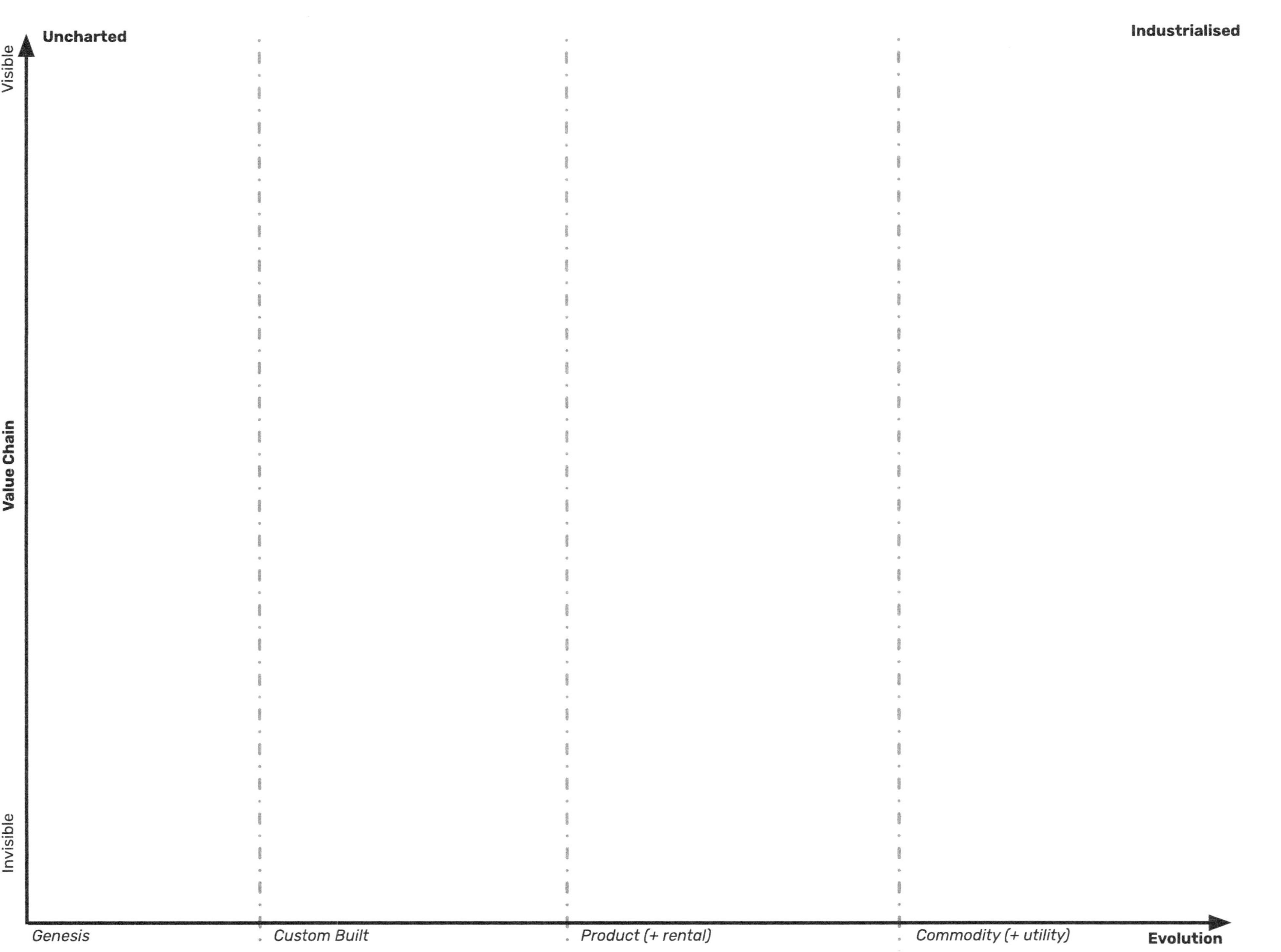
Uncharted
Industrialised
Visible
Value Chain
Invisible
Genesis
Custom Built
Product (+ rental)
Commodity (+ utility)
Evolution

Uncharted

Industrialised

Visible

Value Chain

Invisible

Genesis

Custom Built

Product (+ rental)

Commodity (+ utility)

Evolution

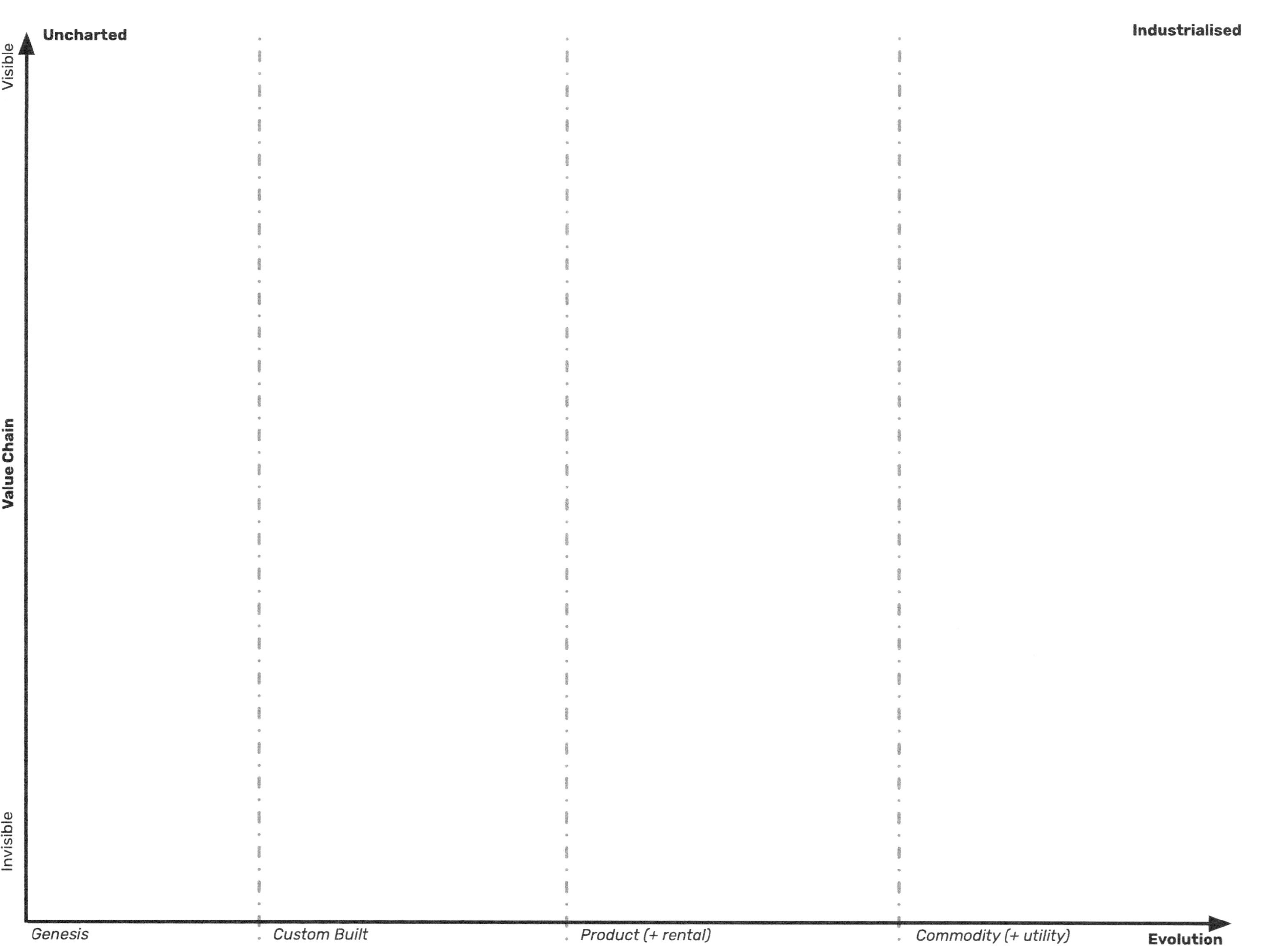
Uncharted
Industrialised
Visible
Value Chain
Invisible
Genesis
Custom Built
Product (+ rental)
Commodity (+ utility)
Evolution

Uncharted

Industrialised

Visible

Value Chain

Invisible

Genesis

Custom Built

Product (+ rental)

Commodity (+ utility)

Evolution

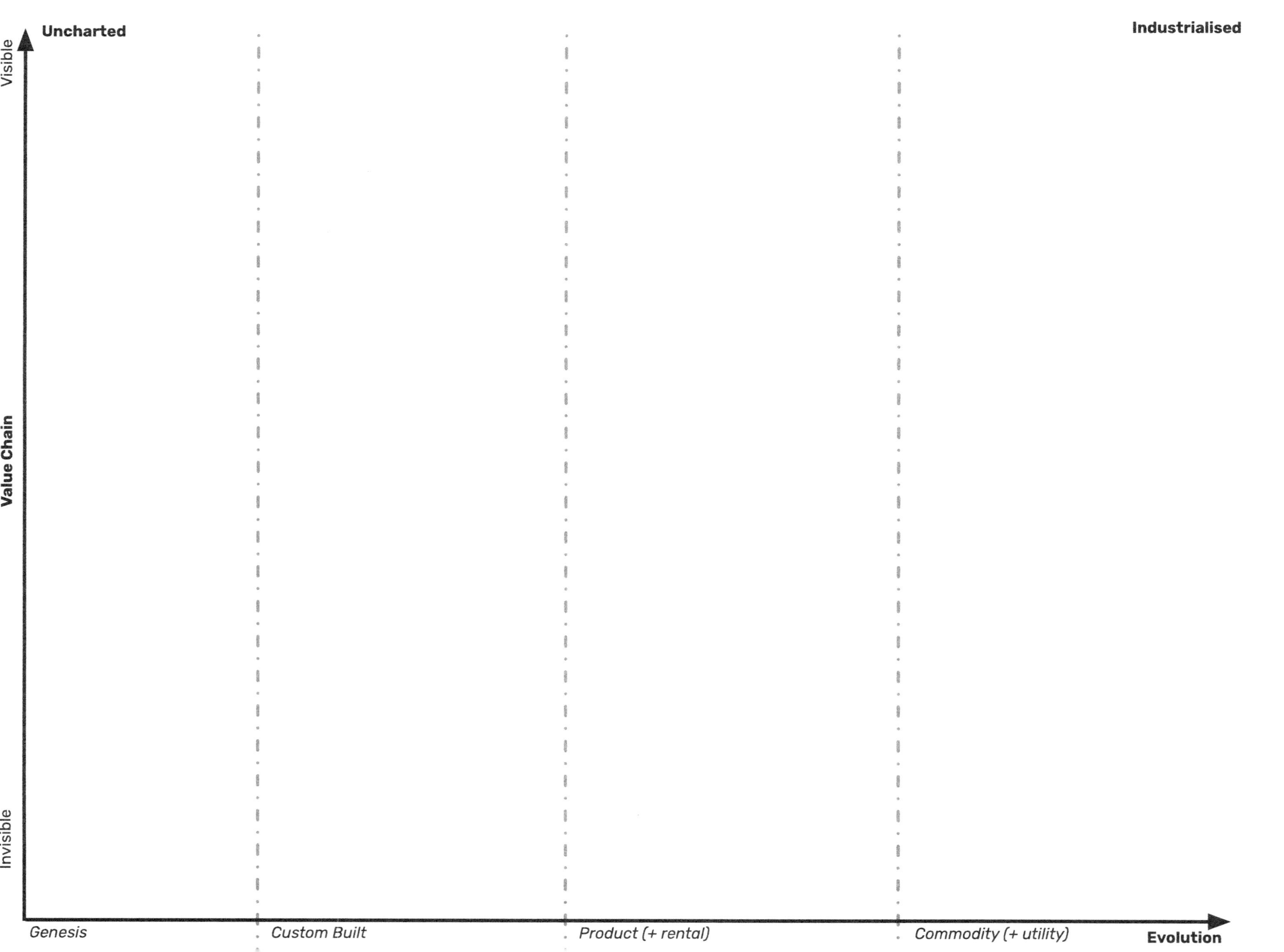

Uncharted
Industrialised
Visible
Value Chain
Invisible
Genesis
Custom Built
Product (+ rental)
Commodity (+ utility)
Evolution

Uncharted

Industrialised

Visible

Value Chain

Invisible

Genesis

Custom Built

Product (+ rental)

Commodity (+ utility)

Evolution

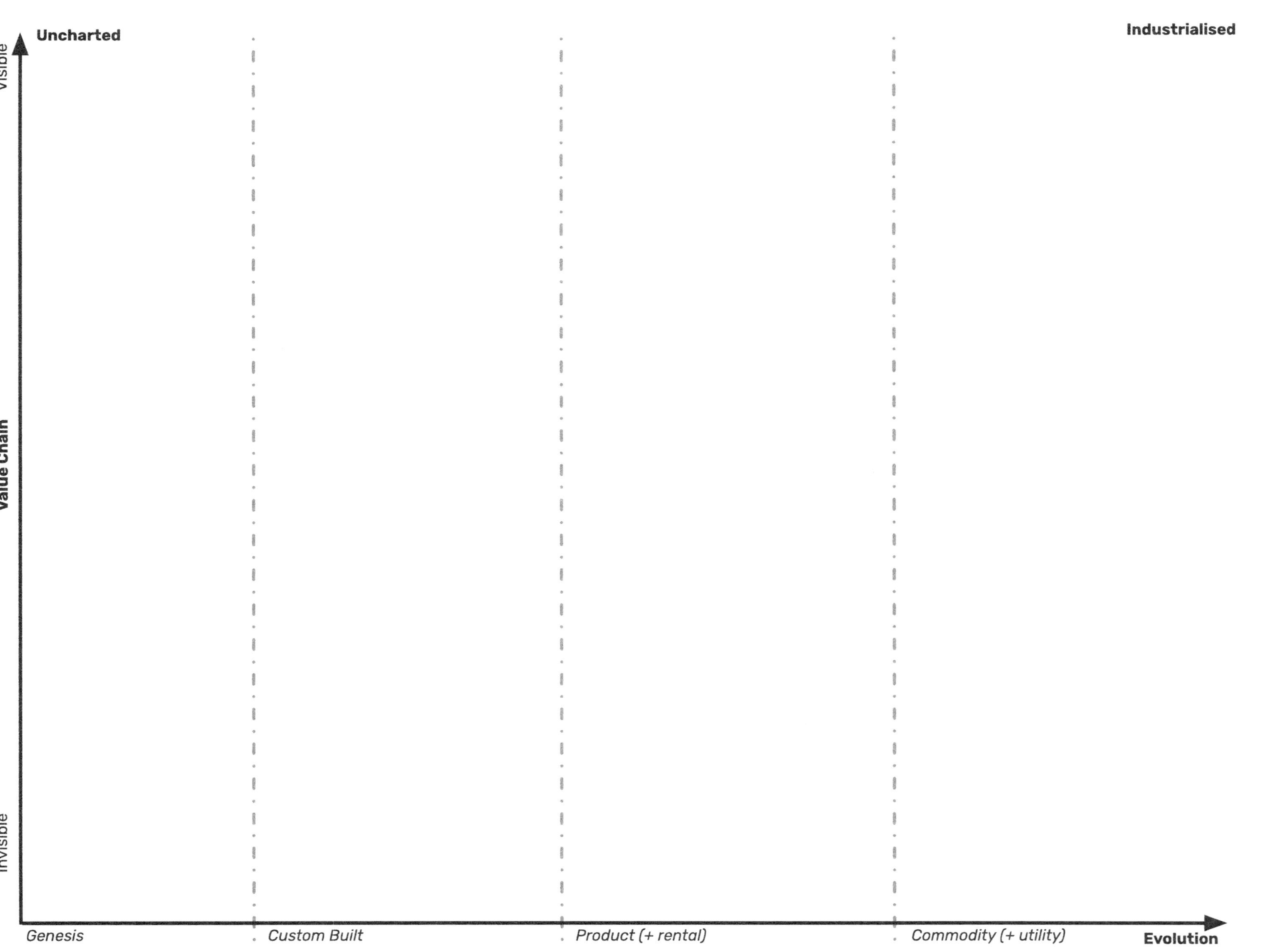
Uncharted
Industrialised
Visible
Value Chain
Invisible
Genesis
Custom Built
Product (+ rental)
Commodity (+ utility)
Evolution

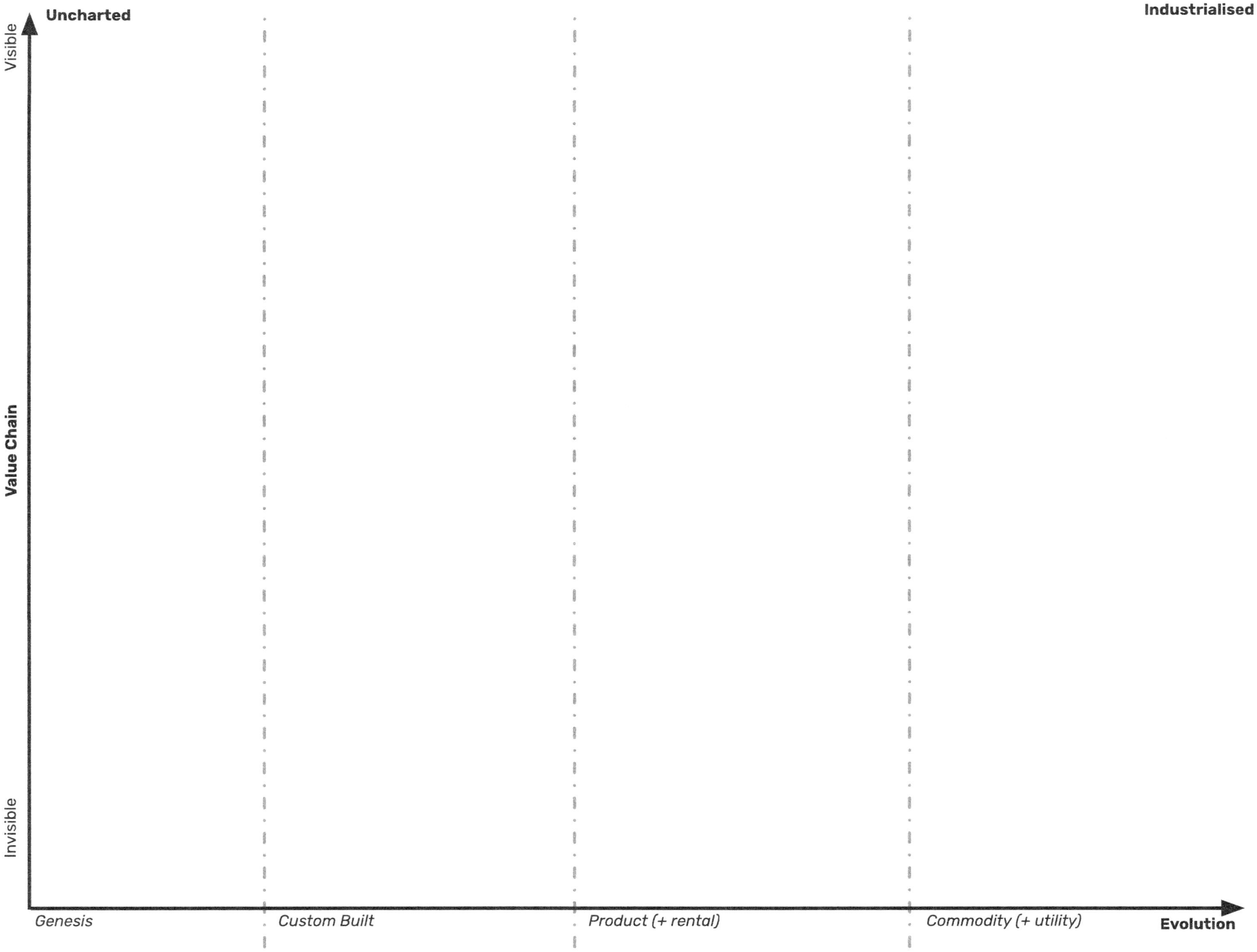

Uncharted

Industrialised

Visible

Value Chain

Invisible

Genesis

Custom Built

Product (+ rental)

Commodity (+ utility)

Evolution

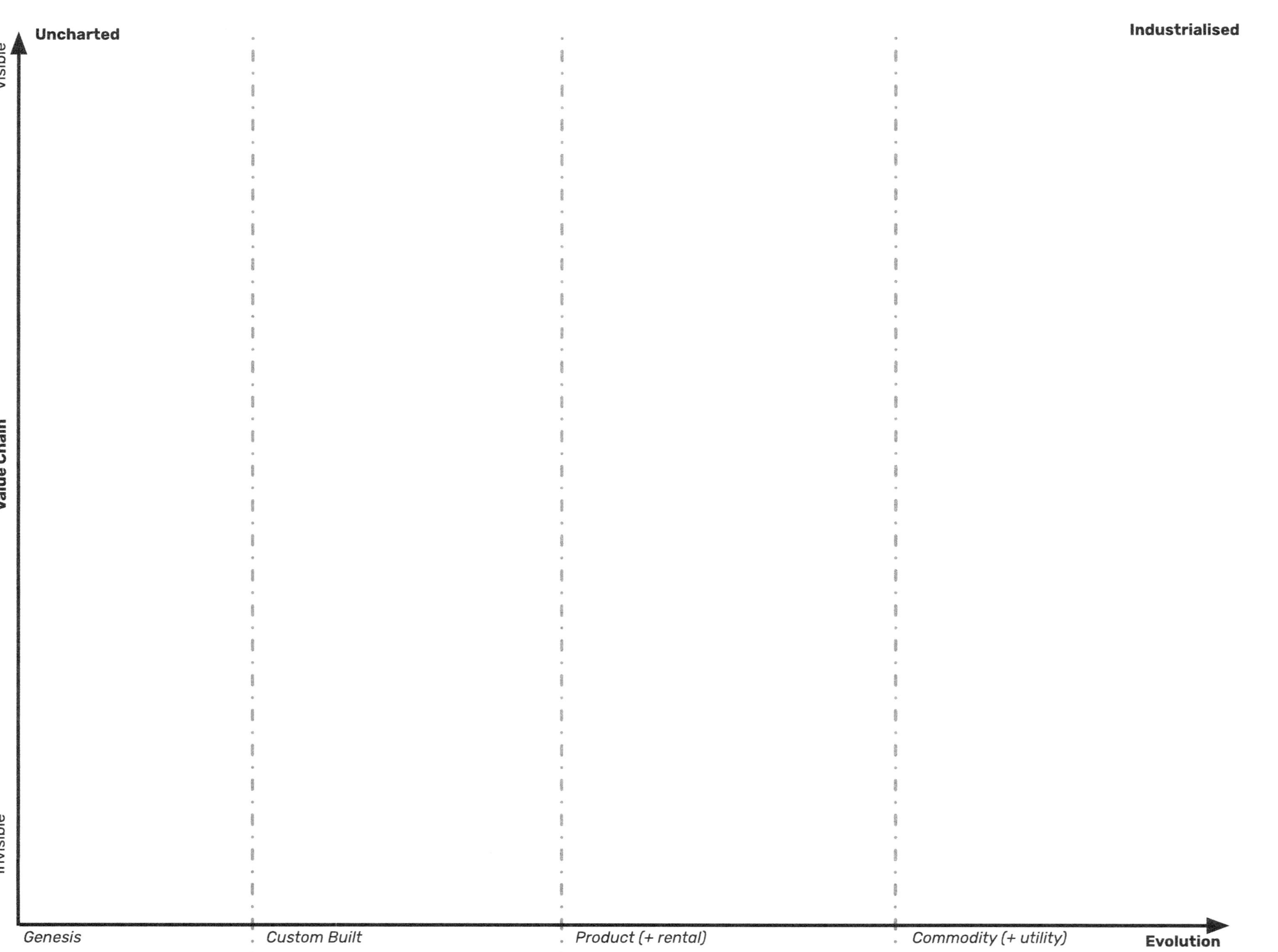
Uncharted
Industrialised
Visible
Value Chain
Invisible
Genesis
Custom Built
Product (+ rental)
Commodity (+ utility)
Evolution

Uncharted

Industrialised

Visible

Value Chain

Invisible

Genesis

Custom Built

Product (+ rental)

Commodity (+ utility)

Evolution

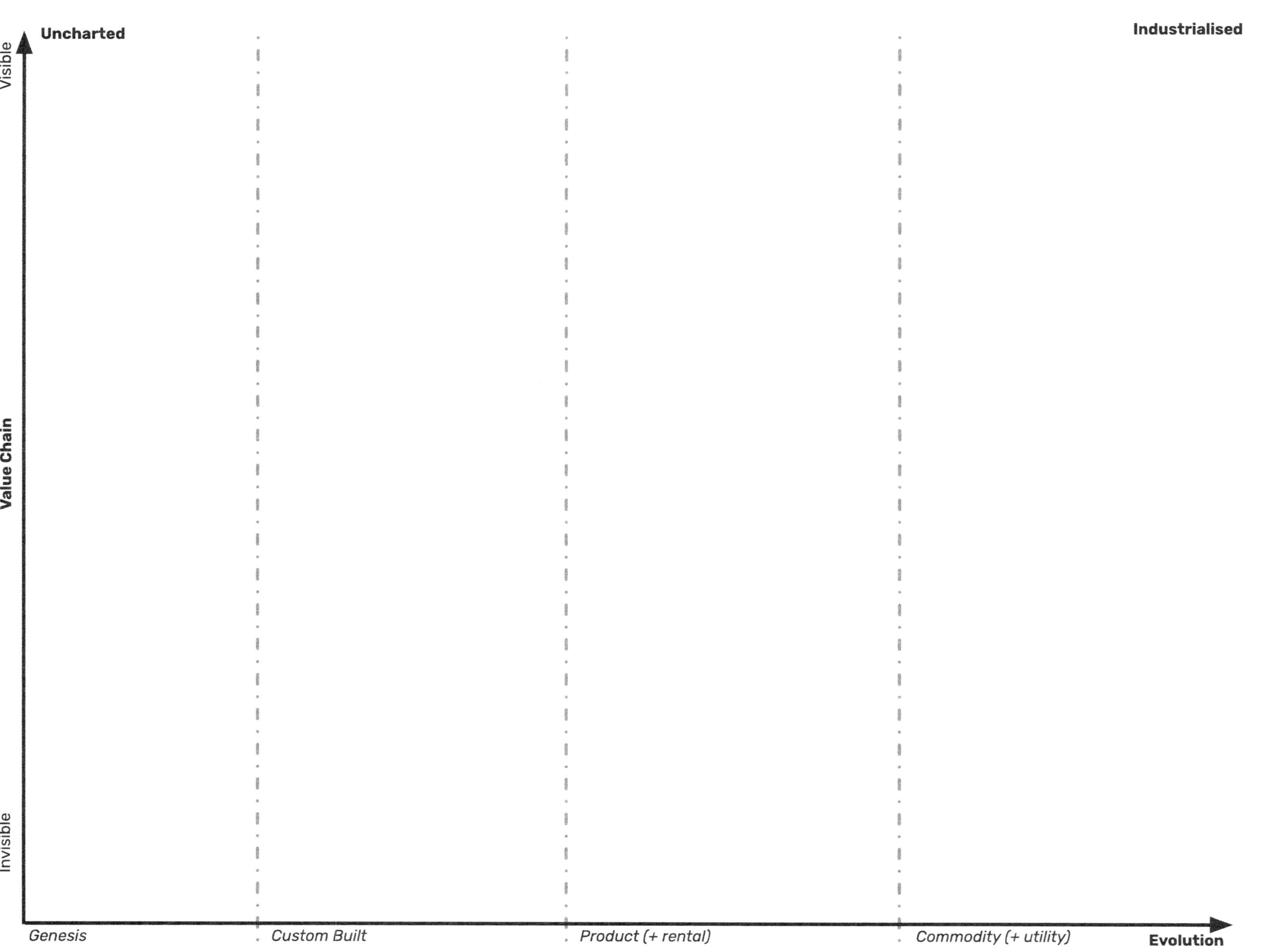
Uncharted
Industrialised
Visible
Value Chain
Invisible
Genesis
Custom Built
Product (+ rental)
Commodity (+ utility)
Evolution

Uncharted

Industrialised

Visible

Value Chain

Invisible

Genesis *Custom Built* *Product (+ rental)* *Commodity (+ utility)* **Evolution**

Uncharted

Industrialised

Visible

Value Chain

Invisible

Genesis

Custom Built

Product (+ rental)

Commodity (+ utility)

Evolution

Uncharted

Industrialised

Visible

Value Chain

Invisible

Genesis

Custom Built

Product (+ rental)

Commodity (+ utility)

Evolution

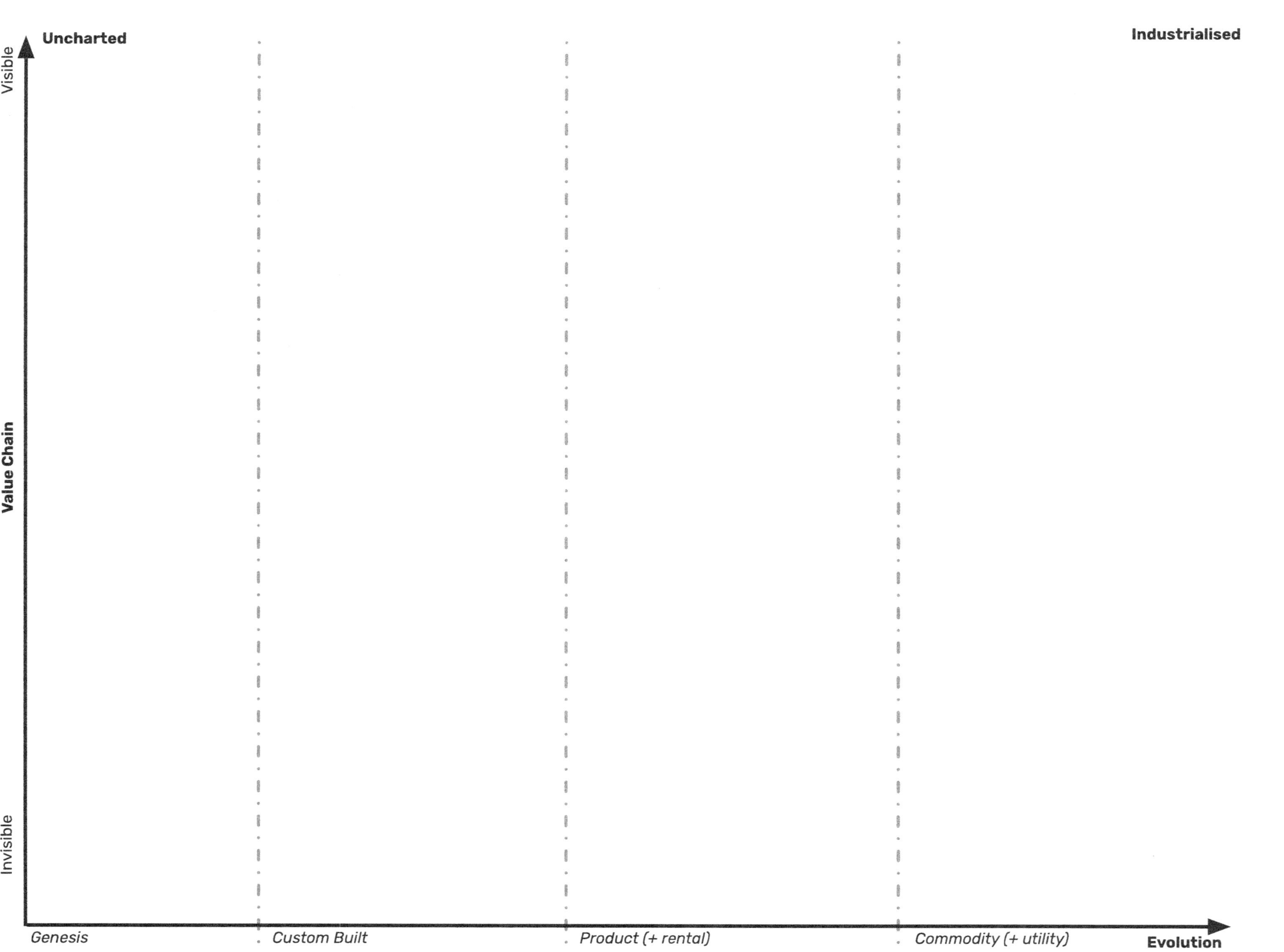
Uncharted
Industrialised
Visible
Value Chain
Invisible
Genesis
Custom Built
Product (+ rental)
Commodity (+ utility)
Evolution

Uncharted **Industrialised**

Visible

Value Chain

Invisible

Genesis *Custom Built* *Product (+ rental)* *Commodity (+ utility)* **Evolution**

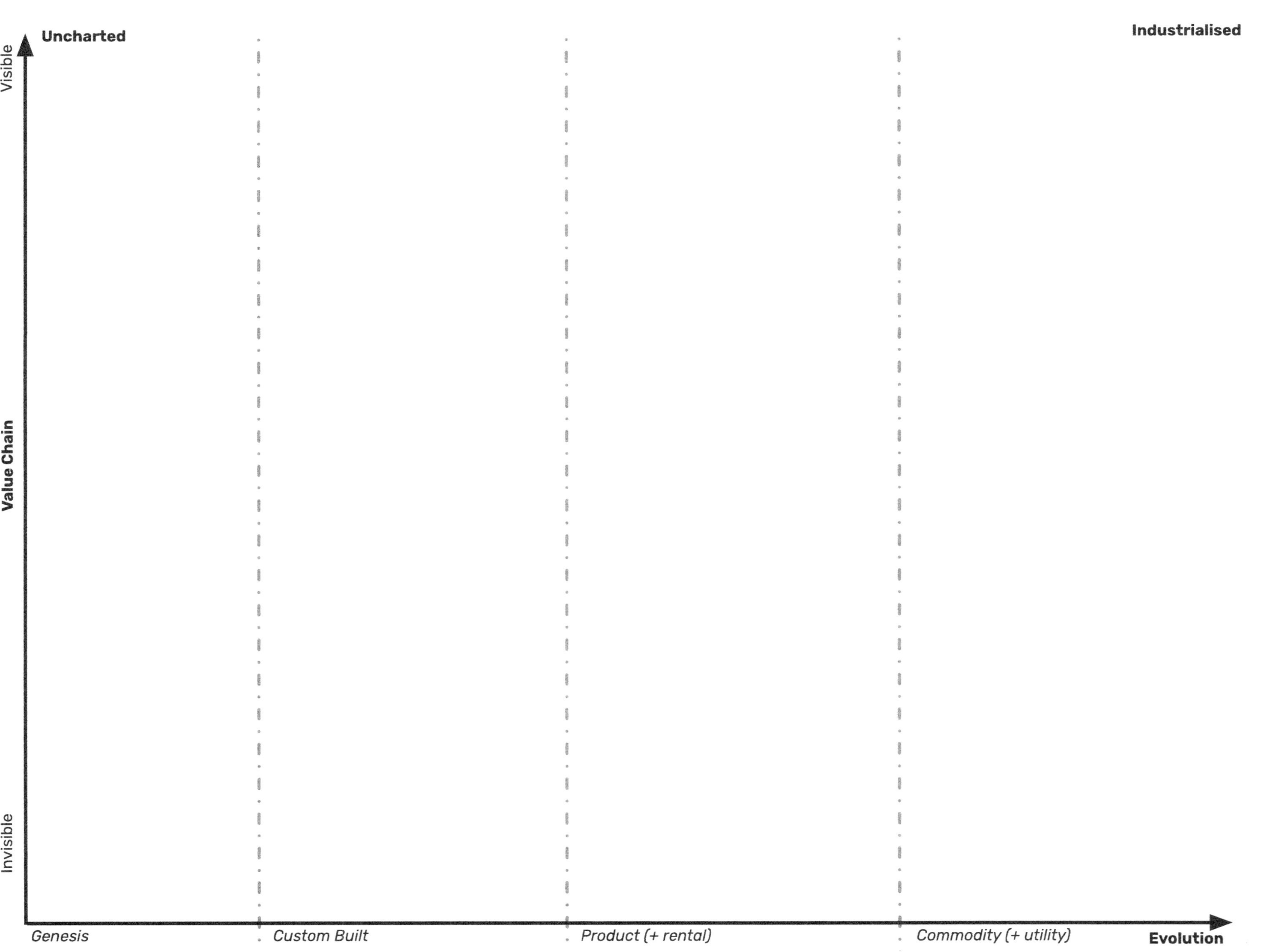
Uncharted
Industrialised
Visible
Value Chain
Invisible
Genesis
Custom Built
Product (+ rental)
Commodity (+ utility)
Evolution

Uncharted

Industrialised

Visible

Value Chain

Invisible

Genesis

Custom Built

Product (+ rental)

Commodity (+ utility)

Evolution

Uncharted

Industrialised

Visible

Value Chain

Invisible

Genesis

Custom Built

Product (+ rental)

Commodity (+ utility)

Evolution

Uncharted

Industrialised

Visible

Value Chain

Invisible

Genesis

Custom Built

Product (+ rental)

Commodity (+ utility)

Evolution

Uncharted

Industrialised

Visible

Value Chain

Invisible

Genesis

Custom Built

Product (+ rental)

Commodity (+ utility)

Evolution

Uncharted

Industrialised

Visible

Value Chain

Invisible

Genesis

Custom Built

Product (+ rental)

Commodity (+ utility)

Evolution

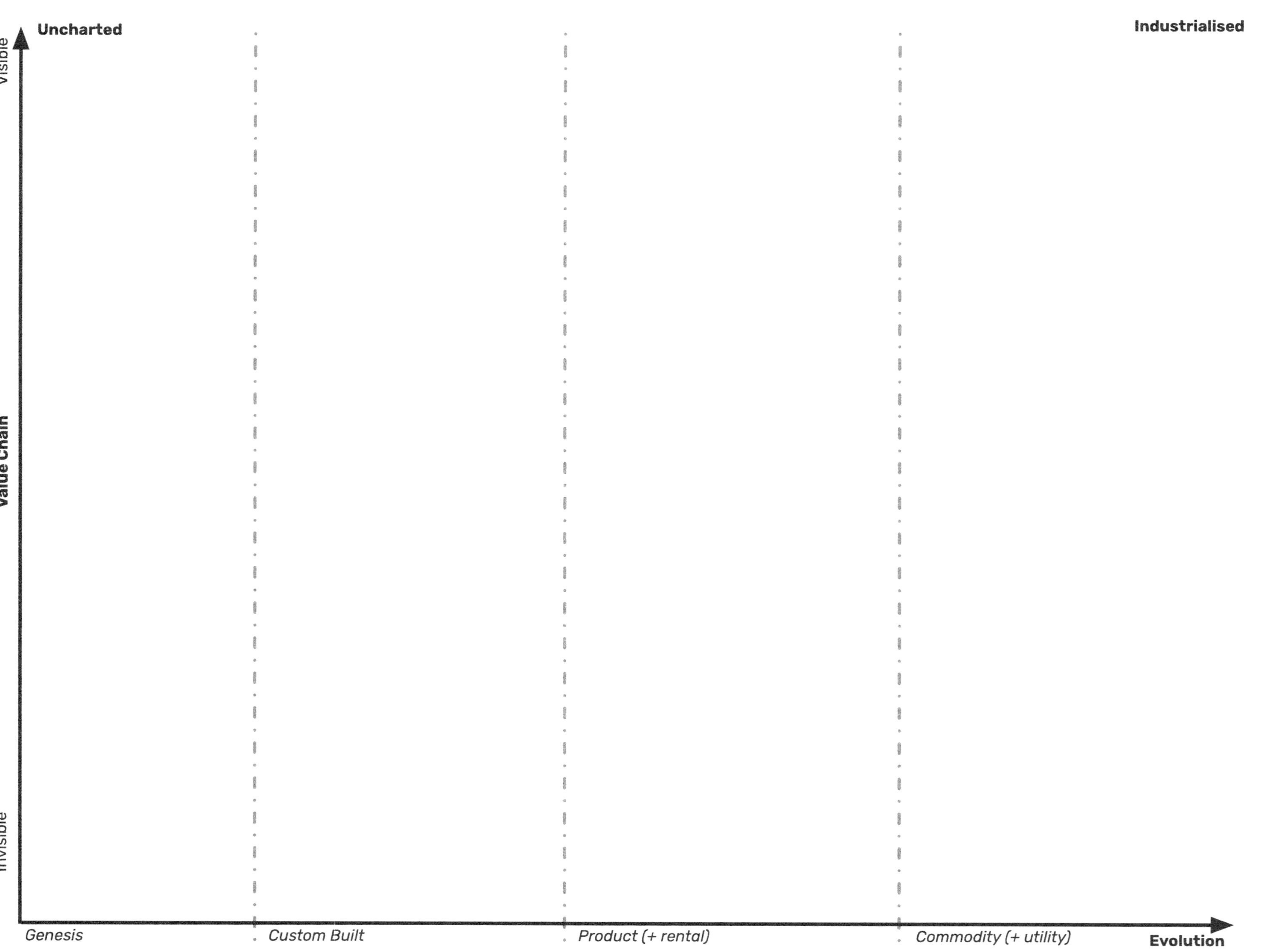

Uncharted
Industrialised
Visible
Value Chain
Invisible
Genesis
Custom Built
Product (+ rental)
Commodity (+ utility)
Evolution

Uncharted

Industrialised

Visible

Value Chain

Invisible

Genesis

Custom Built

Product (+ rental)

Commodity (+ utility)

Evolution

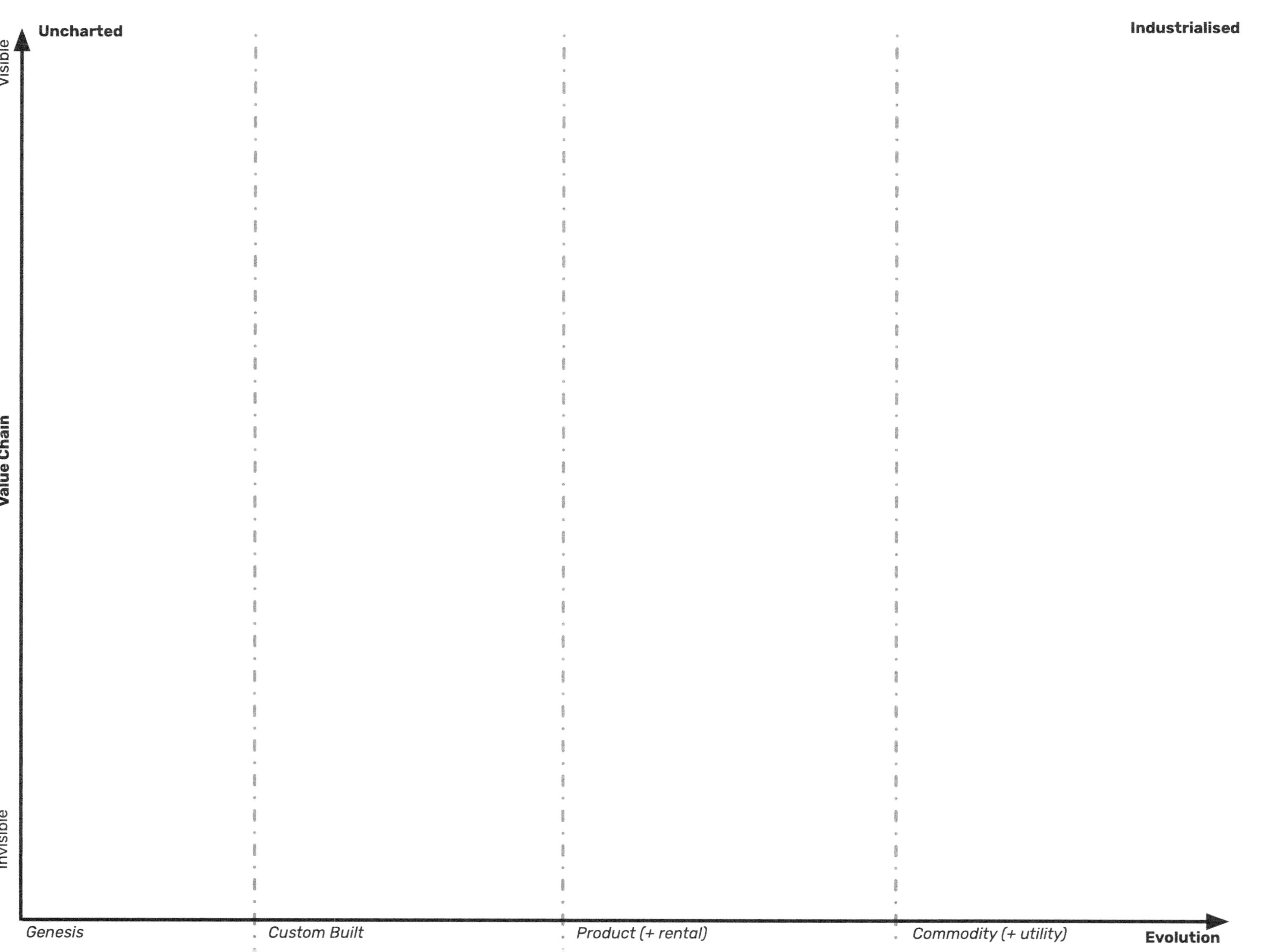
Uncharted
Industrialised
Visible
Value Chain
Invisible
Genesis
Custom Built
Product (+ rental)
Commodity (+ utility)
Evolution

Uncharted
Industrialised
Visible
Value Chain
Invisible
Genesis
Custom Built
Product (+ rental)
Commodity (+ utility)
Evolution

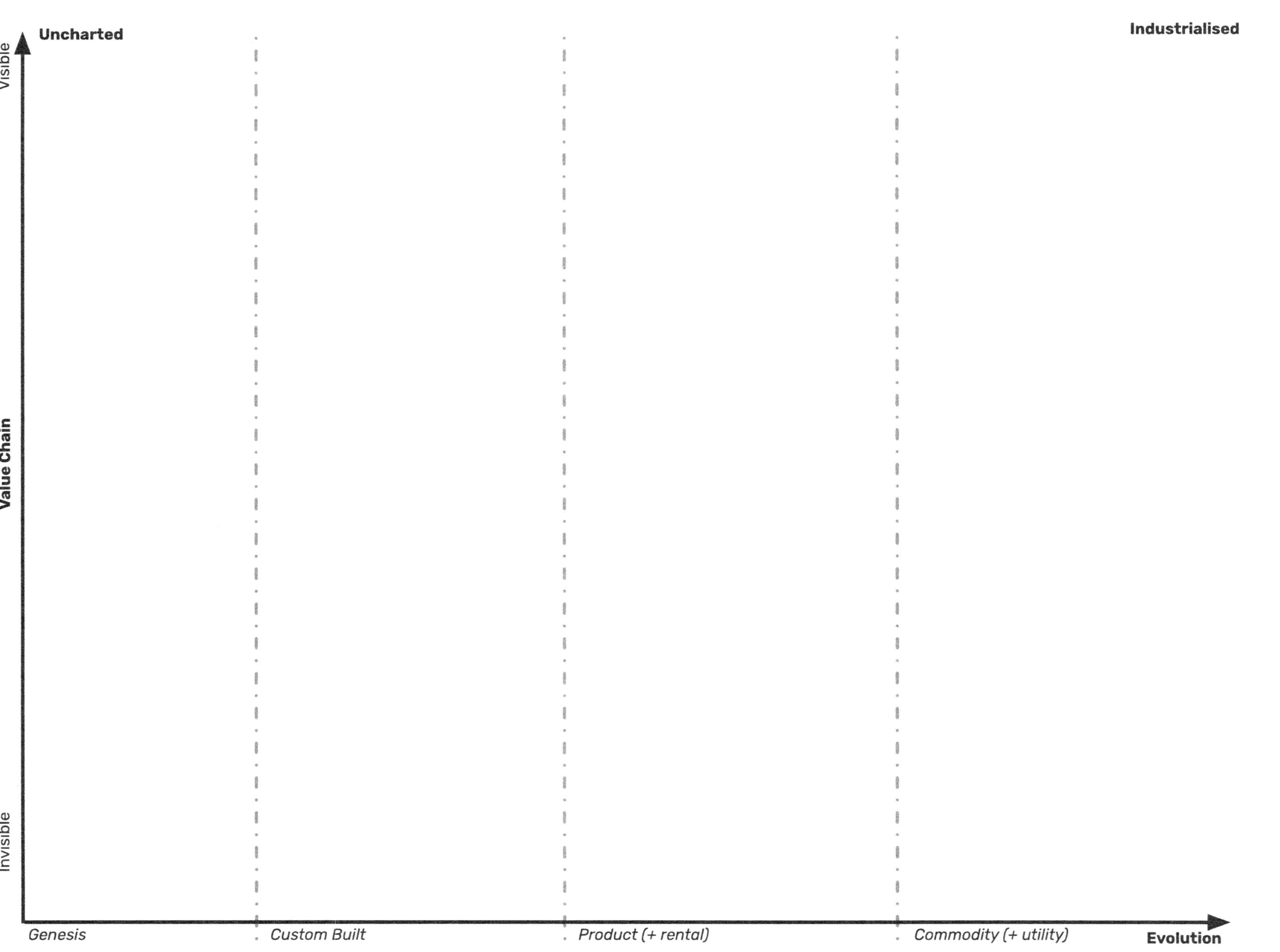
Uncharted
Industrialised
Visible
Value Chain
Invisible
Genesis
Custom Built
Product (+ rental)
Commodity (+ utility)
Evolution

Uncharted

Industrialised

Visible

Value Chain

Invisible

Genesis

Custom Built

Product (+ rental)

Commodity (+ utility)

Evolution

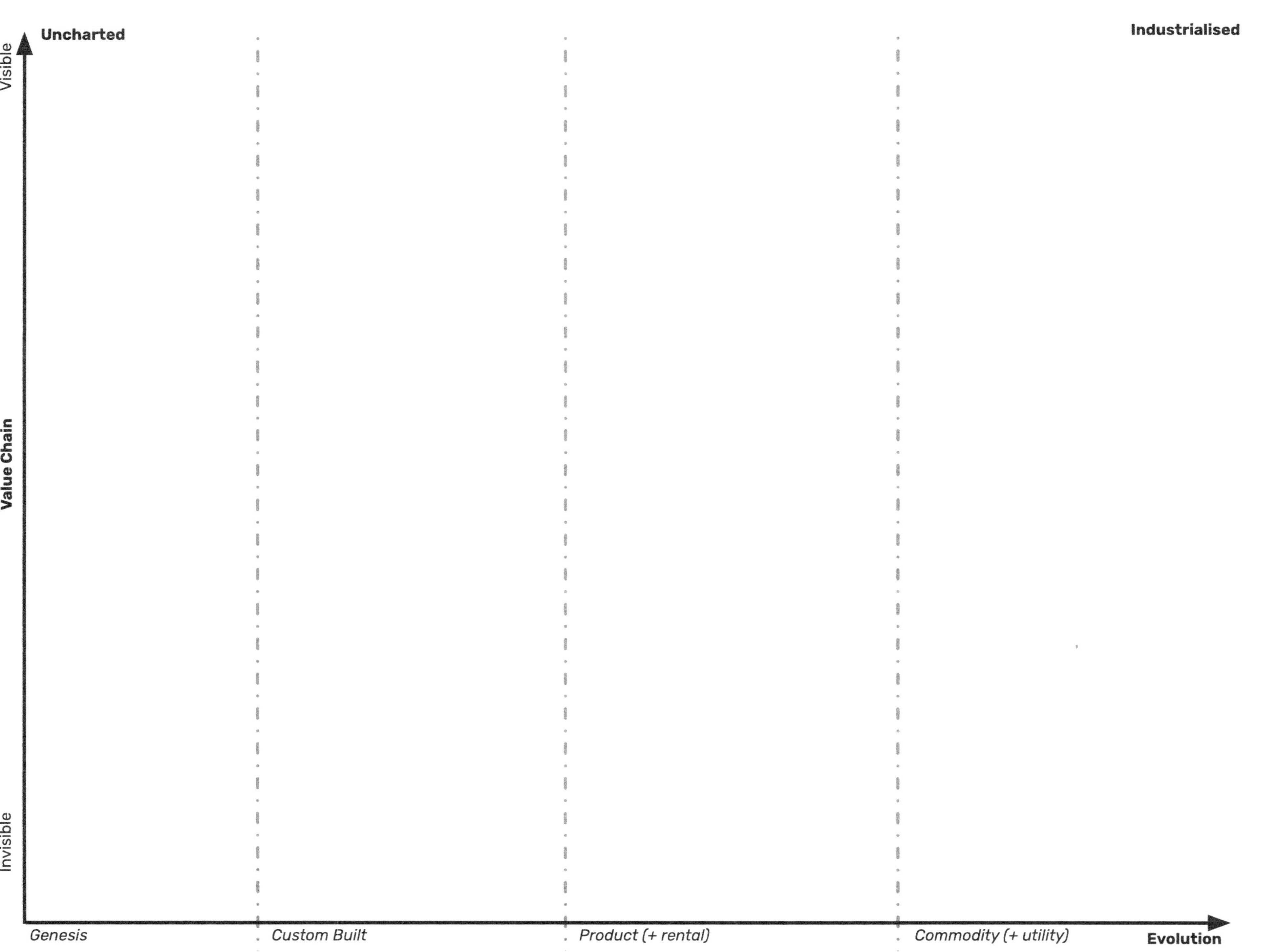
Uncharted
Industrialised
Visible
Value Chain
Invisible
Genesis
Custom Built
Product (+ rental)
Commodity (+ utility)
Evolution

Uncharted

Industrialised

Visible

Value Chain

Invisible

Genesis

Custom Built

Product (+ rental)

Commodity (+ utility)

Evolution

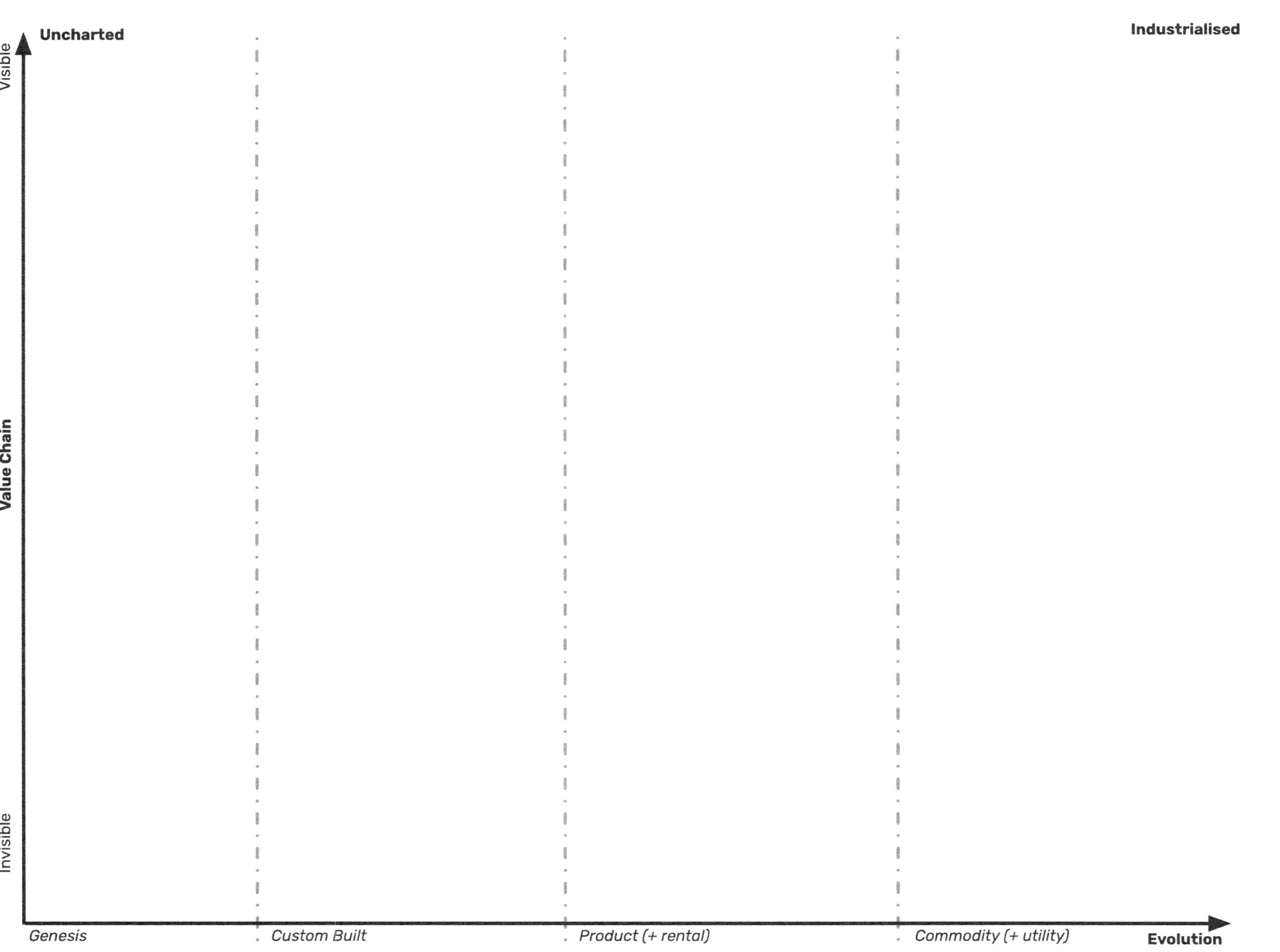

Uncharted
Industrialised
Visible
Value Chain
Invisible
Genesis
Custom Built
Product (+ rental)
Commodity (+ utility)
Evolution

Uncharted

Industrialised

Visible

Value Chain

Invisible

Genesis

Custom Built

Product (+ rental)

Commodity (+ utility)

Evolution

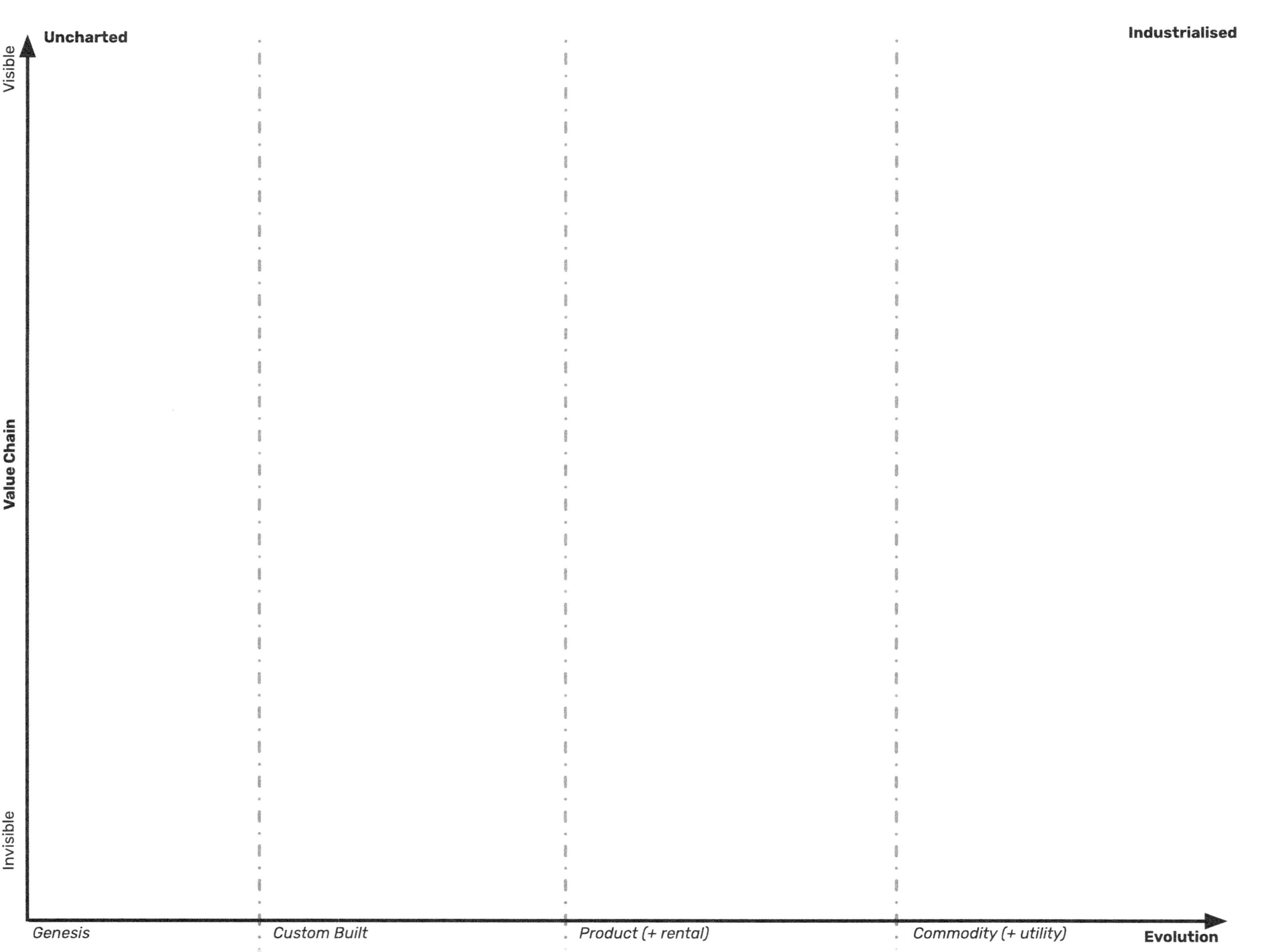
Uncharted
Industrialised
Visible
Value Chain
Invisible
Genesis
Custom Built
Product (+ rental)
Commodity (+ utility)
Evolution

Uncharted

Industrialised

Visible

Value Chain

Invisible

Genesis

Custom Built

Product (+ rental)

Commodity (+ utility)

Evolution

Uncharted **Industrialised**

Visible

Value Chain

Invisible

Genesis *Custom Built* *Product (+ rental)* *Commodity (+ utility)* **Evolution**

Uncharted

Industrialised

Visible

Value Chain

Invisible

Genesis

Custom Built

Product (+ rental)

Commodity (+ utility)

Evolution

Uncharted

Industrialised

Visible

Value Chain

Invisible

Genesis

Custom Built

Product (+ rental)

Commodity (+ utility)

Evolution

Uncharted

Industrialised

Visible

Value Chain

Invisible

Genesis

Custom Built

Product (+ rental)

Commodity (+ utility)

Evolution

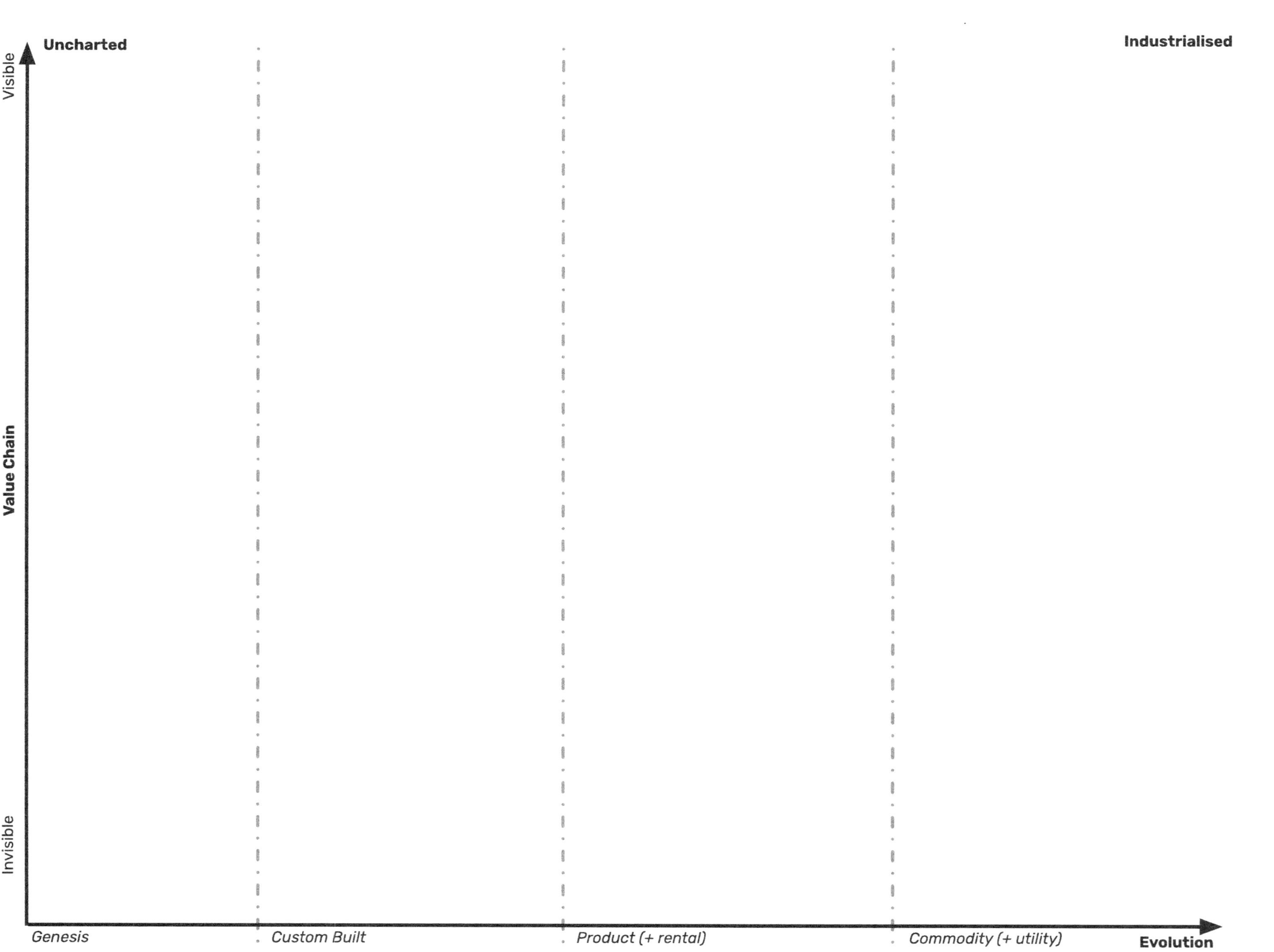

Uncharted
Industrialised
Visible
Value Chain
Invisible
Genesis
Custom Built
Product (+ rental)
Commodity (+ utility)
Evolution

Uncharted

Industrialised

Visible

Value Chain

Invisible

Genesis

Custom Built

Product (+ rental)

Commodity (+ utility)

Evolution

Uncharted

Industrialised

Visible

Value Chain

Invisible

Genesis

Custom Built

Product (+ rental)

Commodity (+ utility)

Evolution

Uncharted

Industrialised

Visible

Value Chain

Invisible

Genesis

Custom Built

Product (+ rental)

Commodity (+ utility)

Evolution

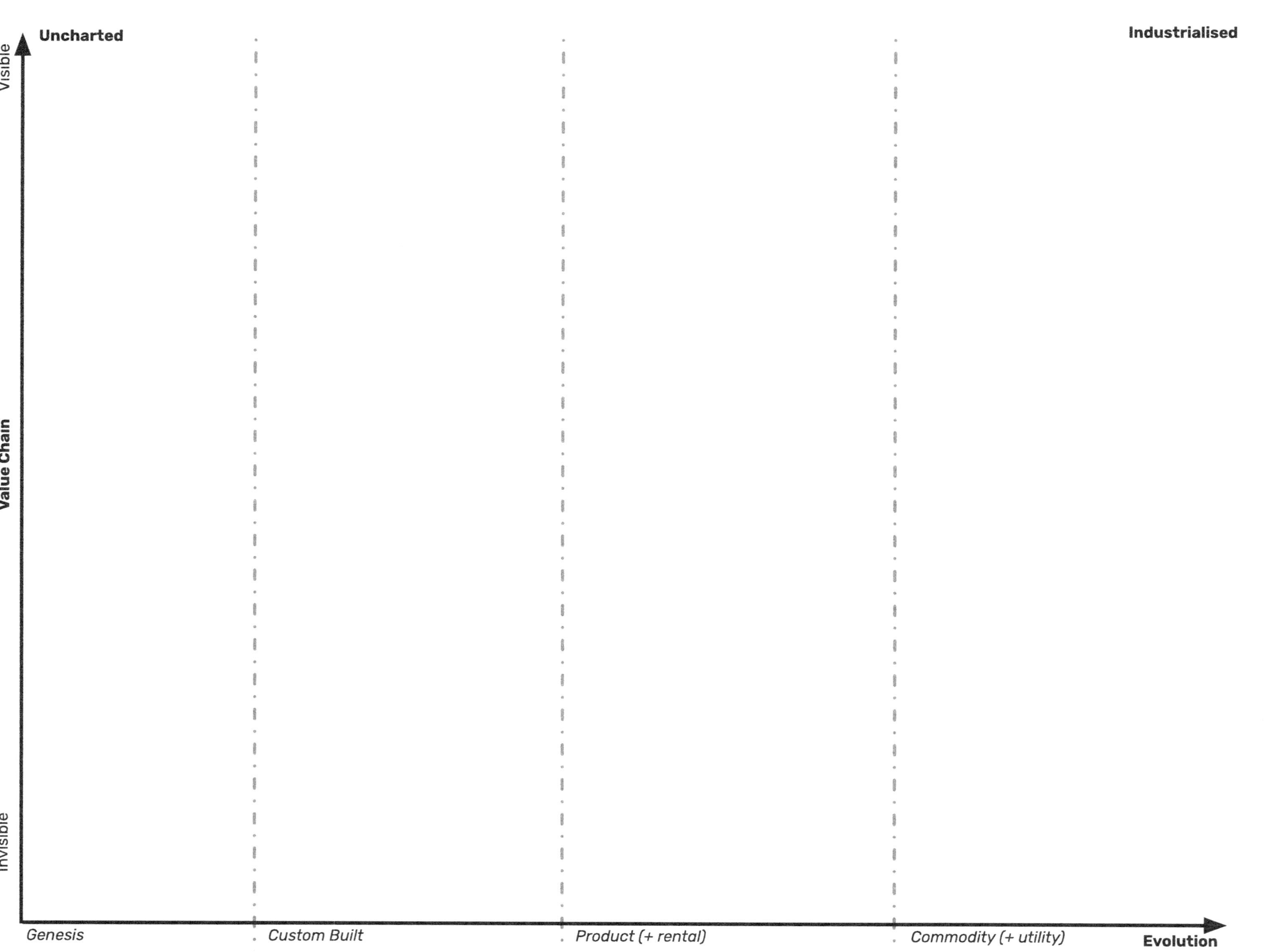
Uncharted
Industrialised
Visible
Value Chain
Invisible
Genesis
Custom Built
Product (+ rental)
Commodity (+ utility)
Evolution

Uncharted

Industrialised

Visible

Value Chain

Invisible

Genesis

Custom Built

Product (+ rental)

Commodity (+ utility)

Evolution

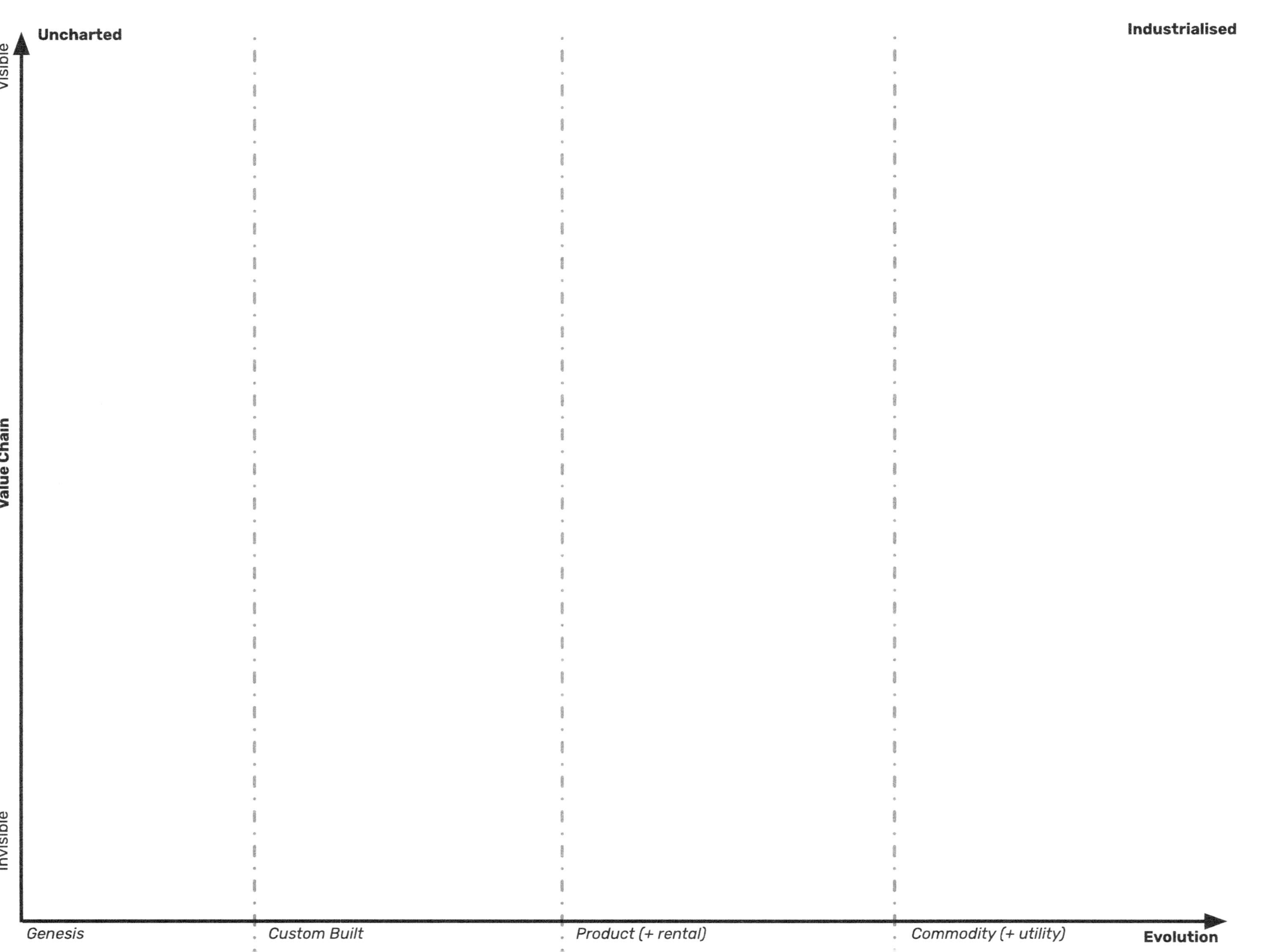
Uncharted
Industrialised
Visible
Value Chain
Invisible
Genesis
Custom Built
Product (+ rental)
Commodity (+ utility)
Evolution

Uncharted

Industrialised

Visible

Value Chain

Invisible

Genesis

Custom Built

Product (+ rental)

Commodity (+ utility)

Evolution

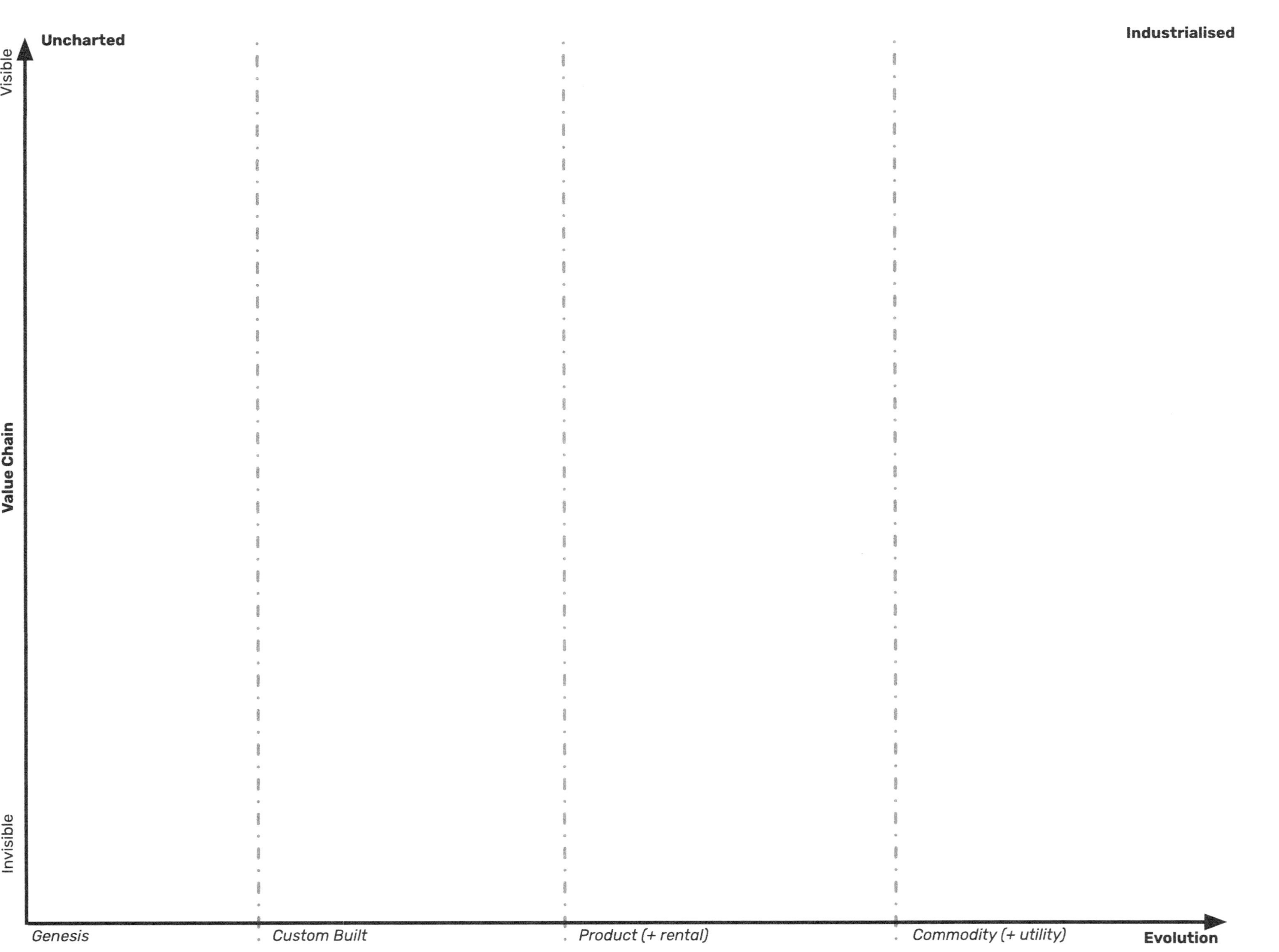
Uncharted
Industrialised
Visible
Value Chain
Invisible
Genesis
Custom Built
Product (+ rental)
Commodity (+ utility)
Evolution

Uncharted

Industrialised

Visible

Value Chain

Invisible

Genesis

Custom Built

Product (+ rental)

Commodity (+ utility)

Evolution

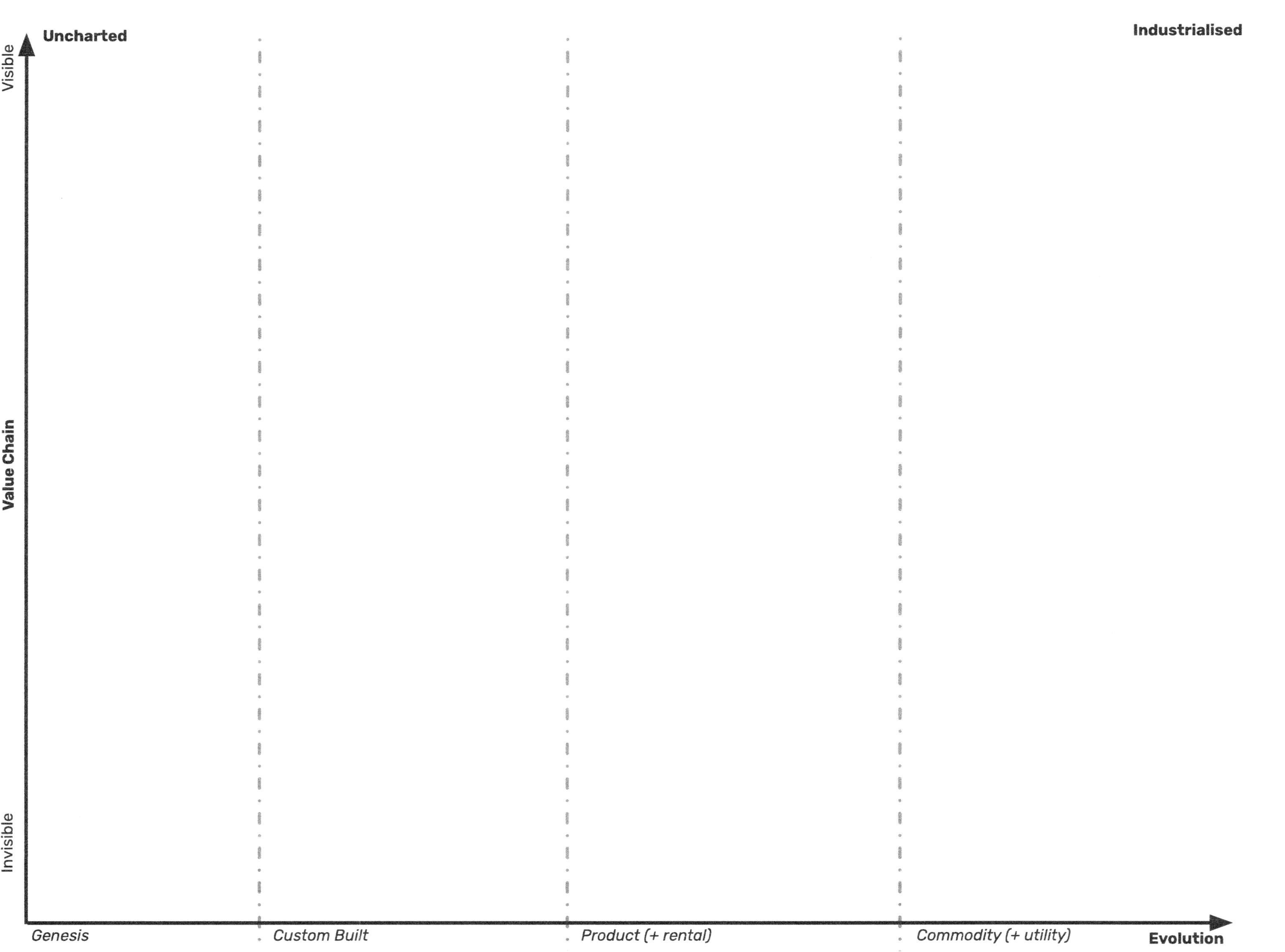
Uncharted
Industrialised
Visible
Value Chain
Invisible
Genesis
Custom Built
Product (+ rental)
Commodity (+ utility)
Evolution

Uncharted

Industrialised

Visible

Value Chain

Invisible

Genesis

Custom Built

Product (+ rental)

Commodity (+ utility)

Evolution

Uncharted

Industrialised

Visible

Value Chain

Invisible

Genesis

Custom Built

Product (+ rental)

Commodity (+ utility)

Evolution

Uncharted

Industrialised

Visible

Value Chain

Invisible

Genesis

Custom Built

Product (+ rental)

Commodity (+ utility)

Evolution

Uncharted

Industrialised

Visible

Value Chain

Invisible

Genesis

Custom Built

Product (+ rental)

Commodity (+ utility)

Evolution

Uncharted

Industrialised

Visible

Value Chain

Invisible

Genesis *Custom Built* *Product (+ rental)* *Commodity (+ utility)*

Evolution

Uncharted

Industrialised

Visible

Value Chain

Invisible

Genesis

Custom Built

Product (+ rental)

Commodity (+ utility)

Evolution

Uncharted

Industrialised

Visible

Value Chain

Invisible

Genesis

Custom Built

Product (+ rental)

Commodity (+ utility)

Evolution

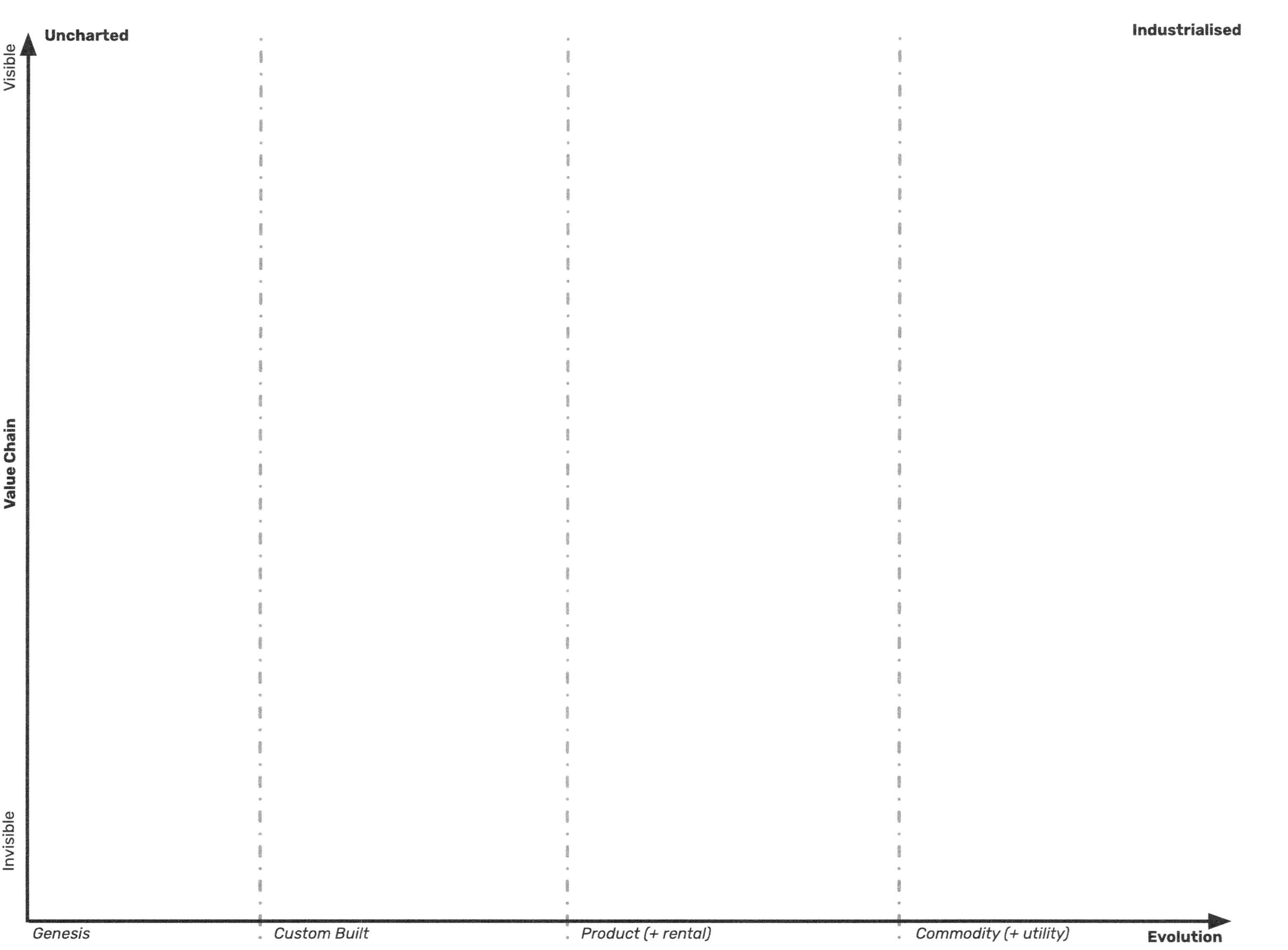
Uncharted
Industrialised
Visible
Value Chain
Invisible
Genesis
Custom Built
Product (+ rental)
Commodity (+ utility)
Evolution

Uncharted

Industrialised

Visible

Value Chain

Invisible

Genesis

Custom Built

Product (+ rental)

Commodity (+ utility)

Evolution

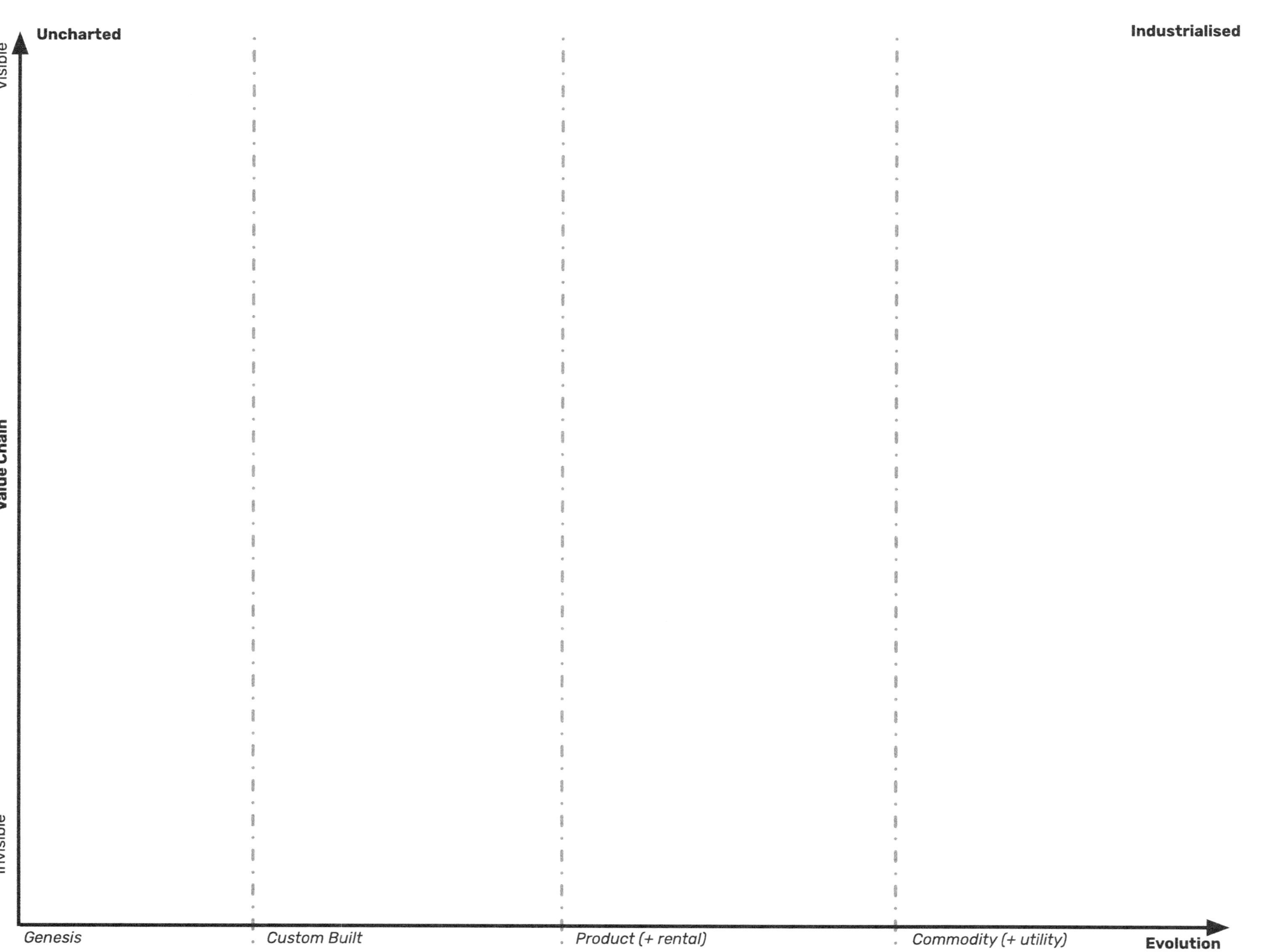
Uncharted
Industrialised
Visible
Value Chain
Invisible
Genesis
Custom Built
Product (+ rental)
Commodity (+ utility)
Evolution

Uncharted

Industrialised

Visible

Value Chain

Invisible

Genesis *Custom Built* *Product (+ rental)* *Commodity (+ utility)* **Evolution**

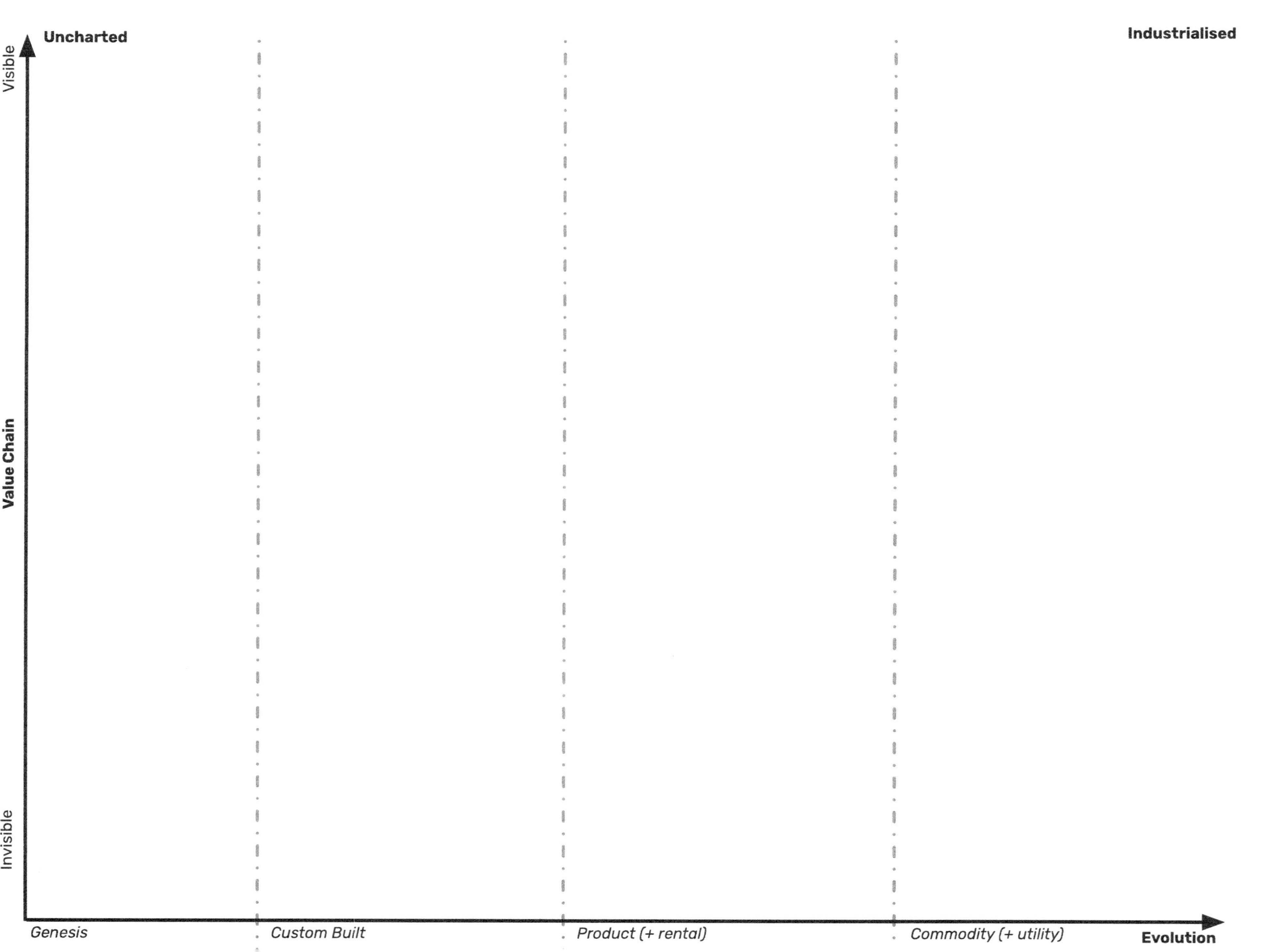
Uncharted
Industrialised
Visible
Value Chain
Invisible
Genesis
Custom Built
Product (+ rental)
Commodity (+ utility)
Evolution

Uncharted

Industrialised

Visible

Value Chain

Invisible

Genesis

Custom Built

Product (+ rental)

Commodity (+ utility)

Evolution

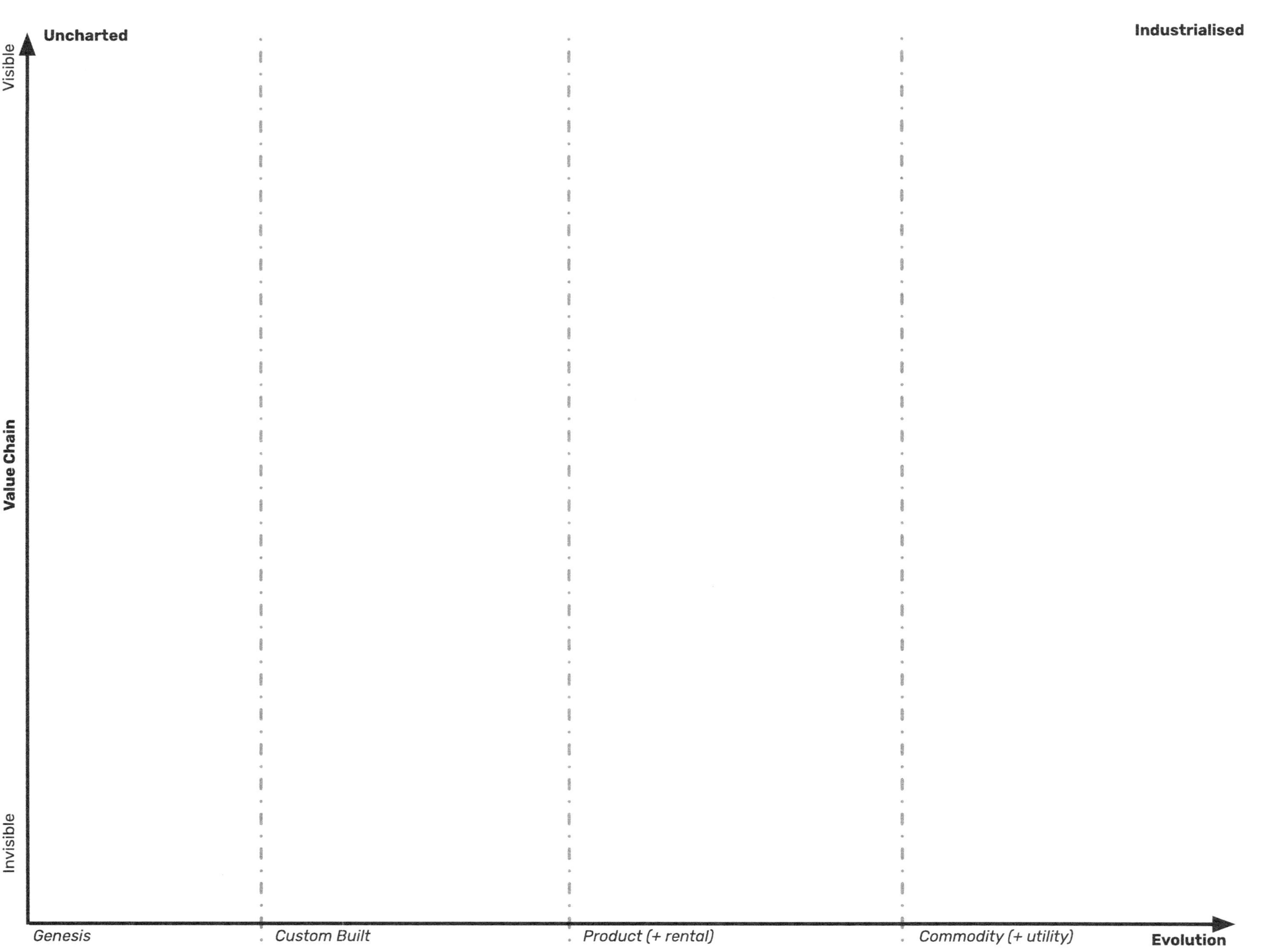
Uncharted
Industrialised
Visible
Value Chain
Invisible
Genesis
Custom Built
Product (+ rental)
Commodity (+ utility)
Evolution

Uncharted **Industrialised**

Visible

Value Chain

Invisible

Genesis *Custom Built* *Product (+ rental)* *Commodity (+ utility)* **Evolution**

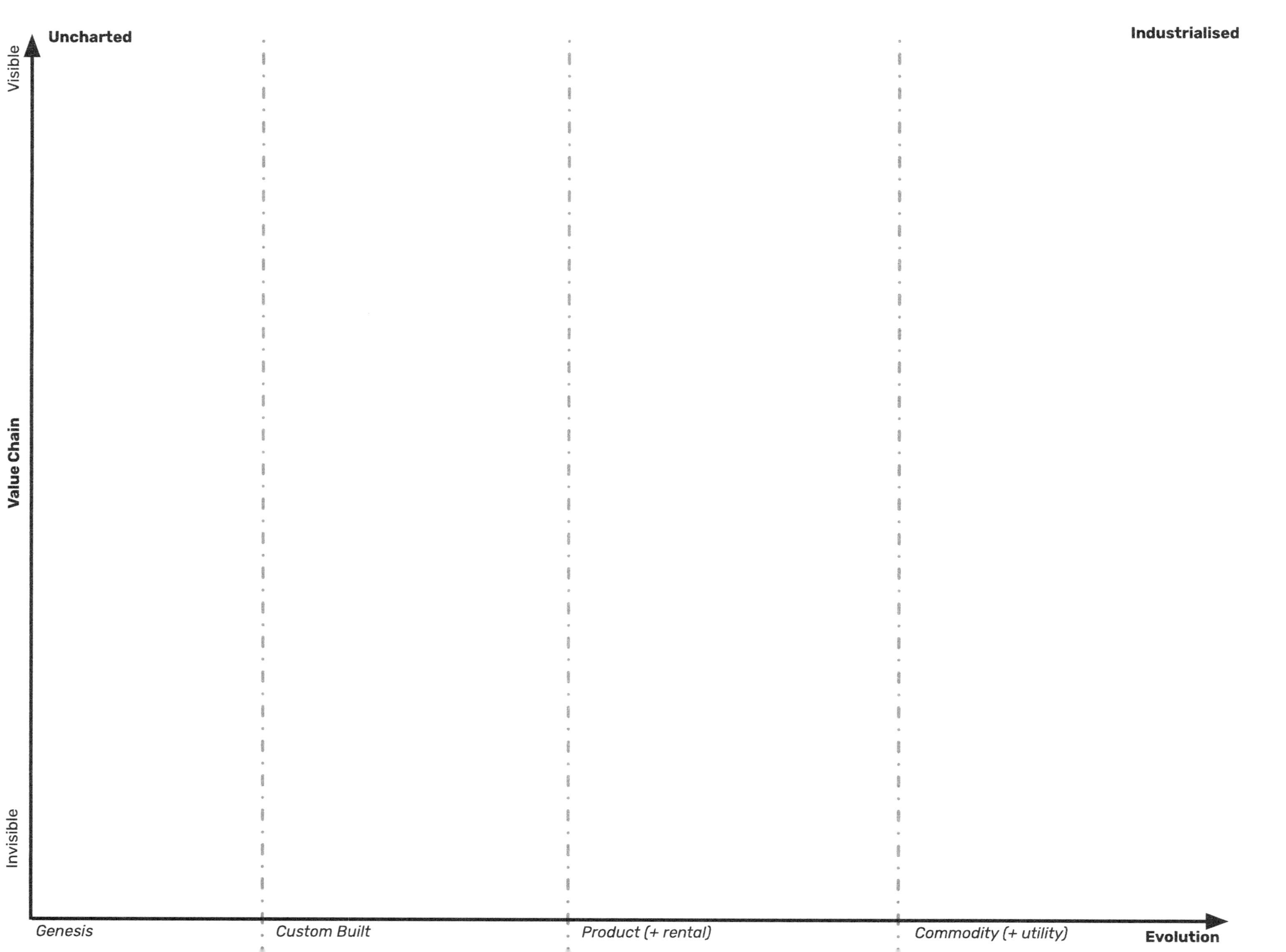
Uncharted
Industrialised
Visible
Value Chain
Invisible
Genesis
Custom Built
Product (+ rental)
Commodity (+ utility)
Evolution

Uncharted
Industrialised
Visible
Value Chain
Invisible
Genesis
Custom Built
Product (+ rental)
Commodity (+ utility)
Evolution

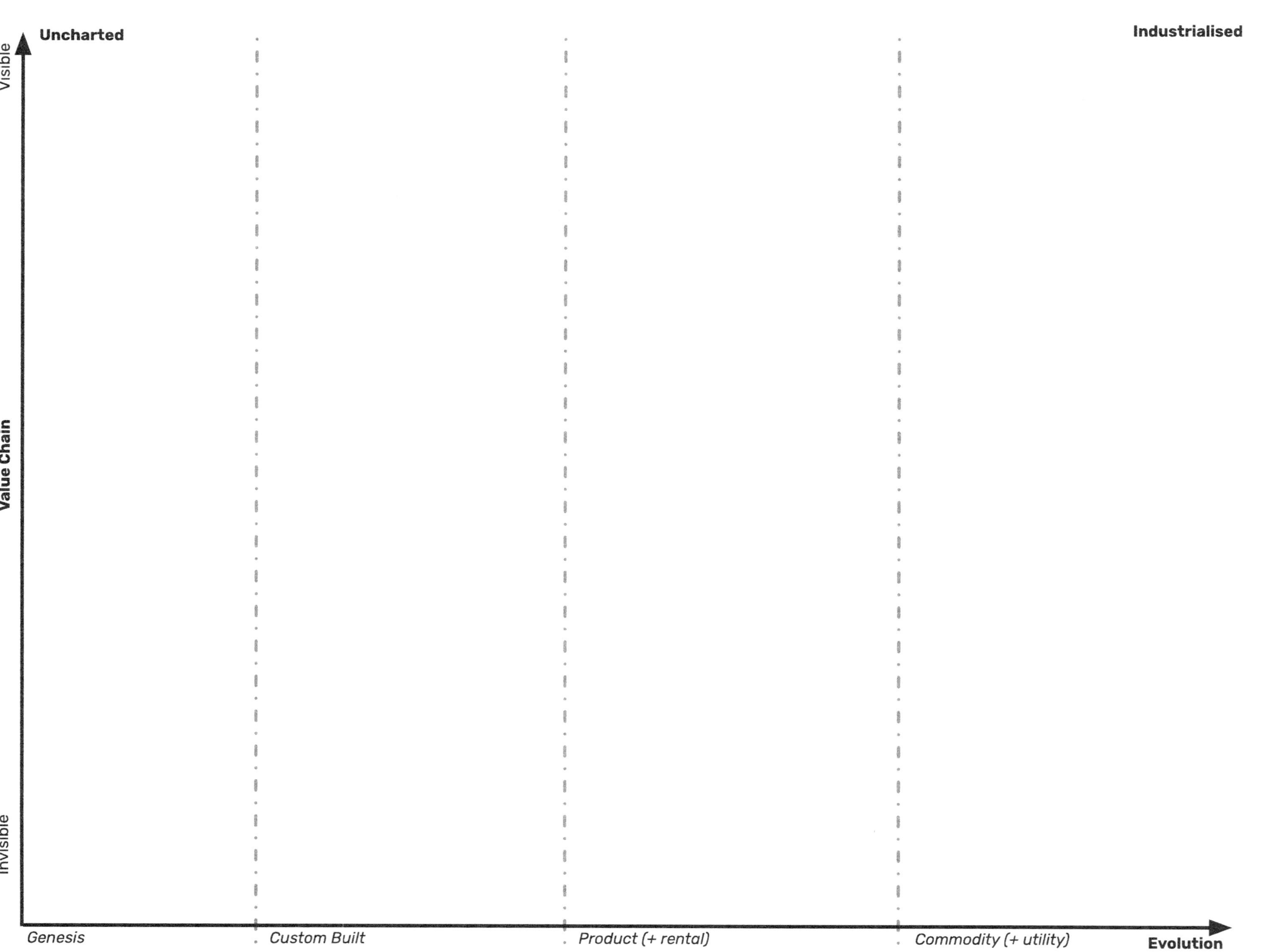
Uncharted
Industrialised
Visible
Value Chain
Invisible
Genesis
Custom Built
Product (+ rental)
Commodity (+ utility)
Evolution

Uncharted

Industrialised

Visible

Value Chain

Invisible

Genesis

Custom Built

Product (+ rental)

Commodity (+ utility)

Evolution

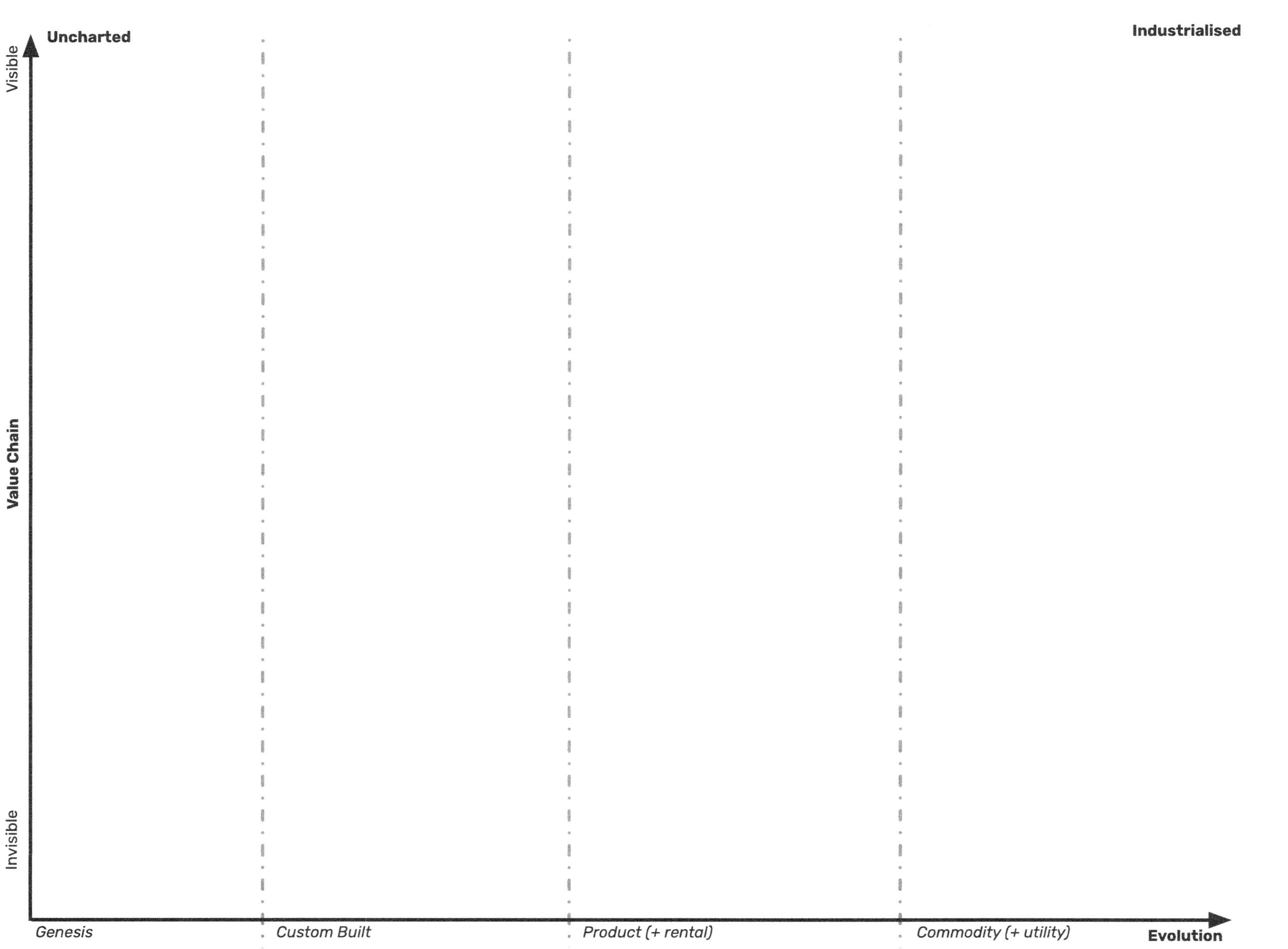
Uncharted
Industrialised
Visible
Value Chain
Invisible
Genesis
Custom Built
Product (+ rental)
Commodity (+ utility)
Evolution

Uncharted

Industrialised

Visible

Value Chain

Invisible

Genesis

Custom Built

Product (+ rental)

Commodity (+ utility)

Evolution

Uncharted

Industrialised

Visible

Value Chain

Invisible

Genesis

Custom Built

Product (+ rental)

Commodity (+ utility)

Evolution

Uncharted

Industrialised

Visible

Value Chain

Invisible

Genesis

Custom Built

Product (+ rental)

Commodity (+ utility)

Evolution

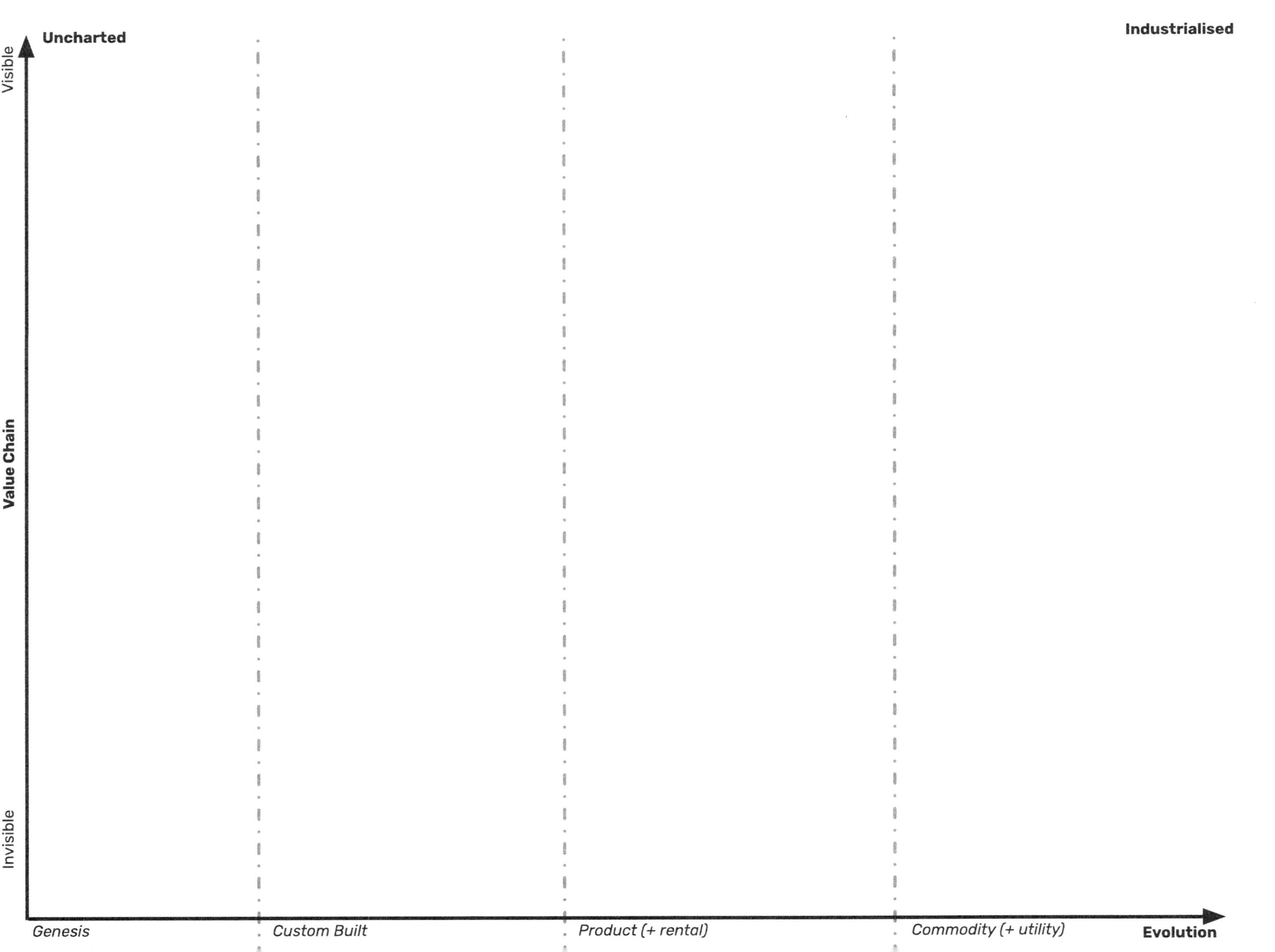
Uncharted
Industrialised
Visible
Value Chain
Invisible
Genesis
Custom Built
Product (+ rental)
Commodity (+ utility)
Evolution

Uncharted **Industrialised**

Visible

Value Chain

Invisible

Genesis *Custom Built* *Product (+ rental)* *Commodity (+ utility)* **Evolution**

Printed in Great Britain
by Amazon

72567823R00061